Navigating

ROUTE
20-
SOMETHING

Erin Keeley Marshall

HARVEST HOUSE PUBLISHERS

EUGENE, OREGON

Cover by Abris, Veneta, Oregon

Published in association with the Books & Such Literary Agency, 52 Mission Circle, Suite 122, PMB 170, Santa Rosa, CA 95409-5370, www.booksandsuch.biz.

NAVIGATING ROUTE 20-SOMETHING
Copyright © 2008 by Erin Keeley Marshall
Published by Harvest House Publishers
Eugene, Oregon 97402
www.harvesthousepublishers.com

Library of Congress Cataloging-in-Publication Data
Marshall, Erin Keeley, 1972-
  Navigating route 20-something / Erin Keeley Marshall.
    p. cm.
  ISBN-13: 978-0-7369-2192-3
  ISBN-10: 0-7369-2192-3
  1. Young adults—Religious life. 2. Young adults—Conduct of life. 3. Marshall, Erin Keeley, 1972- I. Title. II. Title: Navigating route twenty-something.
  BV4529.2.M35 2008
  248.8'4—dc22

                                                    2007028426

Printed in the United States of America

08 09 10 11 12 13 14 15 16 / VP-SK / 11 10 9 8 7 6 5 4 3 2 1

To Steve, with whom I experience the joy
of loving someone more deeply every day.
Thank you for our life together;
you exceed my dreams.
All my love always, always, always.
You can steal my bacon anytime.

Acknowledgments

For filling my life with lessons and love, many thanks to...

Jesus. He's the default answer kids give in Sunday school: When in doubt, answer Jesus. Funny, but it holds a key truth...Jesus is the answer. Thank you, God, for sending him to us and providing the way to you.

Steve...for loving me so well, for being supportive and understanding, and for sharing life with me. I love you so much I don't know what to do with it all.

Paxton E...for being the baby I dreamed of as a little girl playing with dolls. I love you so big and can't wait to see you experience Jesus' love for you.

Dad and Mom...for so much love and nurturing. You two set the bar way high. Thank you for sharing yourselves and your faith early on. You teach me unselfishness.

Dad and Mom M...for raising such a man after God's heart who blesses our family, and for blessing our family yourselves.

Jen, Bryan, Beth, Mark, Mike, Bobbi, Lisa, Leonard, Aaron, and Jaye T...for being my brothers and sisters by blood, by marriage, and by faith. And for being my friends by choice.

Colin, Ethan, Alana, Peyton, Hannah, Sophia, Riley, and Emery...for years of smiles and for being Pax's cousins.

Jennifer and Erin...for LOTS of critiques and encouragement. What a fun couple of years it's been! Many more to come.

Wendy...for being a supportive agent and cheerleader, for signing me, and for believing in the stories of my heart.

Rod, LaRae, and the Harvest House team...for partnering with me on this book and for making it better. It's been a joy and a privilege to work with you.

Contents

Welcome to the Time of Your Life 7

Signposts to Guide Your Way

1. Where are you on the road of life? Driver?
   Passenger? Roadkill? 13

2. Train up your teachability. 19

3. Accept interruptions—the rest is filler. 25

4. Love can take your breath away, but true
   love gives you bigger lungs. 31

5. Dreams worth chasing are worth a
   long-distance run. 39

6. Want the plan? Read the Blueprint. 49

7. Get sure-footed in your own shoes. 57

8. Kill comparison before it kills you. 67

9. Trap your fears or be trapped by them. 75

10. Take it to your knees in prayer. 83

11. Life's messiness didn't end when you
    stopped making mud pies. 89

12. Control the career circus; it's stifling
    inside the tent. 97

13. Everyone has issues; own yours. 107

14. Play it positive. 117

15. Move beyond the pit of regret. 125

16. Shed the stink of unforgiveness. 133

17. Relax and take a load off. .141

18. Lend a hand and help yourself. 149

19. Balance is not just for gymnasts. 157

20. Welcome to the moment; it's disappearing fast. 167

And Then Some

Get Inspired: Quick-Reference Scriptures 177

Make It Matter: 181

Random Suggestions for Living Abundantly

Things I Wish I'd Done More of Sooner

Things I Wish I'd Figured Out Sooner

Things I Wish I'd Seen as Handicaps Sooner

Notes 187

Welcome to the Time of Your Life

No one warned me about the early years of adulthood. Weeks after my twentieth birthday, I road-tripped my way to a new college campus after finishing two years at the local community college. Boxes and crates filled my parents' Buick station wagon from just behind the driver's seat to the far reaches of the way-way backseat (remember those?). Big dreams swirled in my head—or perhaps those were exhaust fumes—while the world waited with bated breath to be amazed by all I would offer it.

Whatever.

Two years later I packed up my cap and gown and left the campus behind for the greener pastures of the real world, only to discover that my naïveté left me somewhat ill-prepared for the countless challenges of the decade to come. Life on my own was more expensive, more demanding, and more uncertain than I had expected. And whaddya know, I wasn't too fond of my first few years as a full-fledged adult.

Maybe your story is working out drastically different. Maybe you've had smooth sailing all the way. You could be one of the rare beings who have never really struggled through friendships, roommate situations, or romantic relationships (or the lack thereof). You may have settled into your dream job right out of the gate and are well on your way up the corporate ladder among a crowd of supportive, honest coworkers whose top priority is your advancement. And you could be raking in the dough faster than you know how to spend it.

Maybe.

But more likely there's been a time or two when the navigation has been tricky or the direction unclear. Chances are you've faced a few patches of choppy water. If not, you will eventually because life is messy no matter how good it is—and it is very good.

Despite all the changes, the first years out of school are full of exciting potential as you arrive on the shore of a vast new world awaiting your unique stamp. I'm only a few years into my thirties, but it's been enough time to take stock of things I wish I'd known that would have made my twenties better. Certain lessons have impacted me in life-changing ways, and I'd like to build on those experiences for as long as I'm around. Perhaps a handful of those insights will help you make the most of these defining years and avoid common pitfalls.

Navigating Route 20-Something: A Lifemap for the Road Ahead takes a thoughtful and sometimes humorous look at 20 views on living I wish I'd taken to heart earlier. Regardless of spiritual background, career path, or marital status, there's something in here for anyone who wants a life full of meaning, free of regret. Each chapter jump-starts conscious thought about approaching every moment with purpose. Examples from God's Word are woven throughout to inspire and challenge, and the follow-up feature "Consider this…" ties in additional Scripture with questions for personal application. Finally, the resources at the end offer a plethora of ideas for making your life matter.

In any season or circumstance we all could use a support network of others who understand what we're dealing with. Therefore, this book is designed for both individual and group use. Rubbing shoulders with peers can provide a platform for rich discussions on a given theme or even important rabbit trails. Depending on your time frame, you can work through the entries one at a time or double up if that fits your schedule.

You have much to offer the world. A wise person once said, "Someone will change the world for someone—will it be you?" If a mediocre existence isn't enough for you, then jump in. It's my prayer that the pages to come will provide a nugget or two of truth to add joy to the journey. This can be the time of your life so far. May it grow fuller by the day.

A fellow traveler,
Erin

I pray that from his glorious, unlimited resources he will empower you with inner strength through his Spirit. Then Christ will make his home in your hearts as you trust in him. Your roots will grow down into God's love and keep you strong. And may you have the power to understand, as all God's people should, how wide, how long, how high, and how deep his love is. May you experience the love of Christ, though it is too great to understand fully. Then you will be made complete with all the fullness of life and power that comes from God. Now all glory to God, who is able, through his mighty power at work within us, to accomplish infinitely more than we might ask or think. Glory to him in the church and in Christ Jesus through all generations forever and ever! Amen.

Ephesians 3:16-21

Signposts to Guide Your Way

WHERE ARE YOU ON THE ROAD OF LIFE?
DRIVER? PASSENGER? ROADKILL?

Okay, so after reading the title of this chapter maybe you're thinking, *Way to go, bummer-girl. Start out with a backfire bang by warning me I might be parked on the side of the road, headed for nowhere?*

Well, yeah, that's one perspective. But what if I told you this road-of-life imagery holds the key to success in life? Don't believe me? It's true. Hang with me for a bit, and you'll see why.

Metaphorically speaking, you are at one of three places all the time.

You may be zooming along in fifth gear, squinting into your rearview mirror at other drivers lagging behind. Job's good, living arrangement is sweet, romance is cooking. Every day is another scenic whirlwind of progress along Route 20-Something.

A second possibility also holds solid potential. You could be riding purposefully next to influential mentors who direct you along a learning curve past road signs that mark the course for you. Still moving forward and gleaning whatever you can along the way, you revel in a landscape of inspiration.

But then there's the third option: the embankment, that slanted part of the road where things get off-kilter. Your engine's kaput and you feel like an obstacle other drivers swerve to avoid—living road-kill, so to speak. It's a tough place to maintain balance and motion; tougher still to keep a clear perspective of the road ahead. Perplexed and depressed, you watch others zoom by, enjoying the career, the spouse, the house. Nothing holds them back.

It's no big secret that life is full of ditches and potholes, and at some point we all will find ourselves in a head-on collision with tough circumstances we just can't seem to steer our way around. Not a fun thought, but better to be forewarned, right? Even if your current journey seems as picture-perfect as a Sunday drive, preparation may reduce the shock factor of tougher times to come.

Wherever you are in life, you have something in common with every other person over 19. You are experiencing firsthand the joys and growing pains of some of your most crucial years. These years are filled with major life decisions and countless opportunities to develop habits and perspectives that could direct your course for the next few decades.

Some of us entered our twenties in a dorm full of birthday hoopla, with friends flocking around wishing us the best. Others of us ventured into this stage of life blessed—or saddled, as the case may be—with a full-time job and a trunkload of responsibility. Who knows? You may even have a spouse or child added to the mix.

No matter how great adulthood can be, it's full of change. And no matter how great change can be, it's unsettling at some level. The twenties revolve around an ever-growing collection of roles—employee, soul mate, parent, leader—that elicit a host of questions, not the least of which is *How do I deal with all this change?*

Here's why this chapter comes first in the book: Our perspectives about the changes, shortcuts, detours, and roadblocks we encounter on the road of life drastically affect the mileage and quality of our journey.

Perspective impacts everything.

Me? I'm one of those who tossed her cap full of dreams and ambitions in the air on graduation day, only to have those aspirations cruise back down to earth with a thud.

But more on that later.

For now, let's get some perspective.

When my life seemed to screech to a halt, my natural instinct was to feel gypped, jealous, inadequate, and impatient. While I worked 18-hour days six days a week, I watched friends land real jobs, find their true loves, and afford places of their own instead of moving back in with the folks. Both my sisters married and finished having babies. Sure, I was happy for them, but I still felt way behind and couldn't help wondering when I'd catch up. Or if I ever would.

If I had a penny for every time I asked God why...or when...or *please!* If only I'd known a life-changing truth earlier in my twenties, how differently I would have viewed those years I thought of as lost time. My level of frustration could have decreased, and my general outlook on life could have been an insurance policy of strength instead of a liability.

The truth I wish I'd known? Here it is:

> *When we let God drive our lives,*
> *there is no such thing as wasted time.*

God has a history of placing people in the wilderness—or at the side of the road, to stick with our metaphor—for the purpose of training them for an incredible role he has planned for their future.

Lightbulb moment: Those stalled seasons are some of the most vital we'll ever experience *if* we focus on what God's goal for them might be. Though ironic or paradoxical, dry times may be even more beneficial to our future than the days and months we spend cruising along from one achievement to the next.

Not convinced? Let's look at a life God appeared to put on hold while he prepared that person for something great—something of immeasurable importance.

The apostle Paul (originally named Saul) was a Jesus hater who hunted down and murdered Christians. But one day God literally stopped him on the road (note the road image) and changed Paul's course (Acts 9:1-31). God loved Paul into becoming one of the greatest missionaries the world has ever known. In fact, Paul wrote several books of the Bible.

Paul was a bold leader, a man of action, someone accustomed to having power. What a shocker it must have been for him to be blind and vulnerable, at the mercy of people he once hated—and who could have harbored hatred against him.

Regardless, once he finally recognized who Jesus was and allowed God to grow him from the inside, Paul couldn't get enough. He pointed his gung ho heart in God's direction, made Jesus his primary concern, and began telling others about the joyful new life he'd discovered.

However, God had a side trip in store for Paul. Here it is straight from Paul: "When this [salvation] happened, I did not rush out to consult with any human being. Nor did I go up to Jerusalem to consult with those who were apostles before I was. Instead, I went away into Arabia, and later returned to the city of Damascus. Then three years later I went to Jerusalem to get to know Peter" (Galatians 1:16-18).

Bible scholars commonly refer to this time as Paul's preparation for ministry. Paul needed training. After all, he had been inundated his whole life with toxic teachings that contradicted the truth that Jesus was indeed the Messiah, the answer to his people's long-running hope of a Savior. Paul had a lot to unlearn and relearn. So God pulled him out of his ministry and planted him in Arabia.

What did Paul do during those three years? He got to know his Savior. He deepened his spiritual roots. He accepted training from above.

Of course, Paul could have spent those years preaching hundreds of sermons; he could have impacted thousands. But God had something more vital to accomplish within Paul first.

Hardly time wasted.

The Bible contains many stories of God rerouting people for a season either for preparation, discipline, or for a greater good. Often for a blend of those reasons.

The Old Testament hero Joseph spent years as a servant, then rose to a high position, got unfairly knocked down again and felt his reputation slung through the mud, spent time in prison, then rose to political power where he showed mercy to his own betraying brothers and saved a nation from famine (Genesis 37:18-36; 39:1–47:27).

The apostle John was exiled to a remote island as a result of his dedication to Jesus. While there, God gave him the visions recorded in the book of Revelation.

And even Jesus himself spent his first three decades of life training for only three years of ministry—but what an impact those years made.

God holds the map with the best route to get us to our ultimate destination, both in this life and for eternity. While his pit stops along the way may appear as abrupt intrusions in our carefully routed geography, there is no dead ground on his road map of life.

Granted, hurts still hurt. Seeking God's perspective doesn't erase disastrous situations, a loved one's betrayal, or a bank balance that refuses to meet expenses. But if we belong to him, we have his assurance that he'll be with us in the middle of any collision. He'll provide the strength we need and will help us get back up and running.

The way we respond to challenges often launches us toward success...or digs us deeper into a hole where we'll continue to spin our wheels. When we're stuck in that kind of rut, we're unable to see the expansive horizon before us.

Rest assured, God wants to show you the best path for you. He wants you to be fulfilled. But sometimes we all need a tune-up before we're ready to handle the road ahead.

Invest yourself in the roadside stops. They are gifts of unmatched scenery for those with hearts sensitized to see them as such.

How's that for perspective?

"I know the plans I have for you," says the LORD.
"They are plans for good and not for disaster,
to give you a future and a hope. In those days
when you pray, I will listen. If you look for
me wholeheartedly, you will find me."

JEREMIAH 29:11-13

CONSIDER THIS...

1. Think back to a circumstance that taught you a life lesson. What happened and what did you learn? How have you been able to apply that knowledge or experience?

2. Do you currently feel like a driver, a passenger, or someone stalled on the side of the road? What circumstances would you change if you could? How does your perspective help or hinder you in your present situation?

3. Read Mark 1:35. When Jesus wanted time alone with God, he purposely went into an isolated place. What does this tell you about where we might find the deepest comfort and closest connection with God?

4. Nehemiah 9:6-25 summarizes the Israelites' history from the time God chose them as his own people, through their suffering as slaves in Egypt, then through their escape, their wilderness time, their repeated rebellion, and their victories in the land God had promised them. Look closely at verses 15-21, which describe God's faithfulness through it all. What do God's mercy and love toward people who constantly rebel lead you to believe about his actions toward those who obey and follow him?

5. How would you describe your relationship with God? What may be holding you back from handing over the controls of your life to him?

TRAIN UP YOUR TEACHABILITY.

Remember the ecstasy of graduation day?

Finals are over, papers turned in, last *i* dotted and last *t* crossed. Your shoulders lift with a newfound lightness as you revel in thoughts of glorious days ahead, unencumbered by projects and term papers and weighty binders of study notes.

Whether this describes your experience last summer or several summers ago, you'll likely recall the sense of freedom you felt knowing you'd never have to step foot in another classroom as long as...

But then one day your rent comes due and reality puts a hitch in your victory dance. And that's just the beginning.

The next morning your alarm doesn't go off, and your late arrival at work is the deciding factor for the promotion you've been eyeing. Your supervisor sends the e-mail congratulating Chris Carefree—the brownnosing schmuck—on a job well done and encourages employees to stop by Chris's new office to offer a pat on the back. You know the office; it was to be your exit from Cubicleland forever. Who cared that it doesn't have a window and you wouldn't have been able to turn around without knocking something over? It's a real *office!*

On the way home you reminisce about the good ol' days when life consisted of term papers and tests. How simple and easy it was.

You stumble into your apartment and dump a dozen plastic grocery bags on the kitchen floor. You shake your arms to revive the circulation and then hit the phone's message button, only to hear that your latest true love has found someone truer. *And* your fish died. *And* lightning fried your computer.

And you thought you'd left the classroom.

Truth is, whether your formal education ended after high school or college, graduation day—commencement, the *beginning*—was merely an entrance into another arena of higher education: the classroom of life. It can be a doozy.

I've noticed an interesting phenomenon. It may not be earthshaking news, but I think it's worth spending a few minutes considering.

I've noticed that lifelong learners are some of the most joyful, successful individuals I've met. They may have struggled through seemingly impossible troubles, overcoming financial disasters, serious illnesses, or any number of other losses, but through it all they continue to ask, *What can I learn in this?*

Learning involves nurturing curiosity, growing from mistakes, being open to finding out we're wrong, and developing a strong measure of bounce-back-ability. Life is a constant learning opportunity. There are no quizzes, no grades, no report cards. Officially, anyway. However, there are tests aplenty requiring our utmost effort. They may be challenges of character and integrity, or strength and endurance. They may strike on any front, whether in a relationship, on the job, at the doctor, through a ministry, or out of the past. Sometimes lessons come from our own errors, while other times we're subject to forces we can't control.

Every person alive faces ups and downs. Look around and you'll see countless ways people have found to cope with the trials and stresses in their unique classroom of life. Sometimes those who've survived the toughest circumstances have the most peaceful countenances, while others who appear to have the world by the tail may come across slightly more cocky or impatient.

You'll surely notice people who embrace negativity and closed-mindedness with every breath they take. They don't seem teachable. And they have no clue just how much they could be cheating themselves.

Think about it. Keeping an open mind and striving to grow through literally every experience validates all of them on some level. The depths of the most tragic loss are filled with rich soil for growing greater compassion and sensitivity. And the most serious mistake can offer a wealth of opportunities to change a habit, deepen a connection, find the truth, and even define one's value system.

That isn't reason to go out and purposely botch a decision or throw caution to the wind; but it's a simple fact that we're going to mess up occasionally, and we're going to come up against tough times. We aren't infallible, and we aren't superheroes. We're faulty, baggage-ridden souls who need help cutting it in an imperfect world. The key is to keep looking for the answers, because the ones who recognize their need and continue to search for help are the ones who will find it. We can bank on that.

John 8:32 says, "You will know the truth, and the truth will set you free." Where is that truth found? Well, Jesus says, "I am the way, the truth, and the life" (John 14:6). Hundreds of years before those words were spoken, God had already told us, "If you look for me wholeheartedly, you will find me" (Jeremiah 29:13). Therein we discover two crucial pieces missing from so many lives: First, Jesus is the help we're ultimately looking for. And second, we are guaranteed to find him if we search earnestly.

Consider this contrast: You may recall the Pharisees, that grumpy group of judgmental religious leaders (whom we love to judge) back in Jesus' day. In John 9, Jesus heals a blind man on the Sabbath, an act equal to heresy in the closed minds of those leaders. True to nature, they're all over his case like fleas on a hound. Far from rejoicing with the healed man who's been given a whole new life, they relentlessly question him and even bring in his parents to verify that he was in fact born blind.

The Pharisees had everything going for them—according to them, anyway: power, education, wealth, status. Naturally, the man is confused that those scriptural scholars have no idea about Jesus' healing power. "'Why, that's very strange!' the man replied. 'He healed my eyes, and yet you don't know where he comes from? We know that God doesn't listen to sinners, but he is ready to hear those who worship him and do his will. Ever since the world began, no one has been able to open the eyes of someone born blind. If this man were not from God, he couldn't do it.'"

Their response says a lot about them. "'You were born a total sinner!' they answered. 'Are you trying to teach us?' And they threw him out of the synagogue" (verses 30-34). Their unteachable natures kept them from learning an essential eternal truth.

Jesus later finds the man—and the Pharisees—and clarifies things a bit further by telling him, "I entered this world to render judgment—to give sight to the blind and to show those who think they see that they are blind."

The Pharisees demand to know if Jesus is calling them blind, to which he says, "If you were blind, you wouldn't be guilty...But you remain guilty because you claim to see" (verses 39-41).

Imagine their fury!

Pharisees are still around today. I recognize them in myself more often than I'd like to admit. I gripe and groan about things I don't understand or can't control, berating myself for my inadequacies, ignoring the obvious, or refusing to admit to poor judgment. When I'm like that, my real problem is not the problem itself; rather, it's my reaction to the problem.

Those who are willing to learn, who have seeking spirits, are some of the happiest people around. They are the ones I want to be like, for they do life well no matter what. They embody the most encompassing definition of success because their success is not dependant on circumstances, but rather on the growth they invite with their teachable spirits.

Teachable people accept their own limitations, welcome correction, and continue to seek the One who offers the answers.

How's the learning environment in the classroom of your life?

Don't bother correcting mockers; they will only hate you.
But correct the wise, and they will love you.
Instruct the wise, and they will be even wiser.
Teach the righteous, and they will learn even more.
Fear of the LORD is the foundation of wisdom.
Knowledge of the Holy One results in good judgment.

PROVERBS 9:8-10

CONSIDER THIS...

1. In general, is it harder for you to 1) admit your mistakes, 2) come to terms with your limitations, or 3) accept that you can't control all the details?

2. Think back to a circumstance that taught you a life lesson. What happened and what did you learn? How have you been able to apply that knowledge or experience?

3. What does Hebrews 5:11-14 say about continuing to grow?

4. What's the source of wisdom, and what part does it play in being teachable? Psalm 51:6; 86:11; John 14:6; Colossians 3:16; and 2 Timothy 3:16-17 shed light on this question.

5. According to Psalm 94:12; Matthew 11:28-30; and Romans 15:4, what are some benefits of being open to what God wants to teach you? Consider current struggles in your life. How might those benefits help you through these circumstances?

3

ACCEPT INTERRUPTIONS—
THE REST IS FILLER.

I had a dentist appointment this morning.

At least that's what the ink said on my Day-Timer's eight a.m. slot. But as the hand on the reception area's wall clock inched past that time, my frustration grew.

A row of magazines overlapped on the coffee table, and I flipped through a *People,* not really caring about the latest Tinseltown scoop. Twenty minutes later I'd long since gotten my fill of Hollywood gossip when a woman opened the outside door and joined me across the room. We ignored each other.

Tick-tick-tick.

The door to the exam area finally swung open, and an assistant smiled to my co-waiter and motioned for her to come.

Huh?

The morning's Bible study lesson on fruit of the Spirit flitted through my brain. *Okay, no biggie,* I rationalized. *Perfect opportunity to practice some of that fruit. Peace, patience…long-suffering.* Unfortunately, my blood pressure didn't care much about spiritual produce at the moment.

It turns out there was no record of my appointment. "Tiffany" had been working when I scheduled it six months ago, and apparently it was not her first glitch.

I rescheduled the appointment, patted myself on the back for my ever-so-gracious response to the receptionist's apology, and returned to my car.

As I pulled out of the parking lot, the lid on my annoyance cracked open just enough to let my brain run through all the ways they'd done me wrong. *Thirty*-minute drive. *Thirty*-minute wait. *And another thirty-minute drive.*

Didn't they know I had important work to do? I had a devotional to write! A Bible study to complete!

Aren't you impressed?

Knowledge and application are not synonymous, and I have not yet mastered the skill of appreciating life's interruptions. Looks like some lessons are slower to take root.

If there's always more on your to-do list than space allotted in your planner, perhaps you'll relate to my frustration this morning. Imagine waiting 30 whole minutes. Horror.

But as hindsight is wont to do, it brought a contrasting perspective to my initial take on the situation. I arrived home and eased off my high horse...and the quiet nudges began to hit. They're the not-so-subtle messages from the Holy Spirit that let me know I've missed the goal. Familiar with those?

Well, those nudges were telling me I'd missed *something*. Unable to ignore them, I let them run their introspective course through my thoughts. Sure enough, they had a word for me.

Blinders.

Oh brother, those again. More often than not, I put on an imaginary set of blinders when I dress for the day. And while they serve a good purpose in keeping me focused, oftentimes they block out important events around me and narrow my scope on the rest of the world. Typically, if I'm put off by an interruption, it's because I'm wearing blinders.

Suddenly my morning bout of self-righteous indignation seemed more like spoiled brattiness. Or modern frenzy run amok.

I covet my time. I know this, but all too often my heart still grips the controls. After all, it's *my* time, right? My schedule, my to-do list, my Day-Timer. I'd been single long enough to assume that freedom of time was one of the perks of life on my own. I'd gotten spoiled by that misconception.

So now I'm married, and I've traded some perks for others. My husband and I have a say in each other's time. Okay, that's fine; definitely worth the minor loss of independence. Steve and I are both driven, self-motivated overachievers, a shared trait that works for us. Up before the sun, we each have our well-ordered routine before breakfast at 6:00.

However, while those characteristics and habits are all fine in and of themselves, both of us can describe occasions when our task-oriented natures caused us to miss out on quality moments with people and serendipitous moments with God.

Take my commute home this morning. Imagine the conversation I could have enjoyed with God, the insights he may have wanted to reveal to me, had I focused my energy off of that boondoggle at the dentist and trained my thoughts onto him and the beautiful day he was unfolding around me. And it was a truly amazing day. Blue sky, perfect temperature, gentle breeze—the whole shebang.

As I meandered through the Land of Retrospect, it occurred to me that the receptionist may have been facing some *real* concerns. I'll never know what a smiling face could have done for her. I could have been a thermostat instead of a thermometer, setting a pleasant temperature for her day instead of reacting to the unwelcome cloud I saw in my own—a cloud that actually held a refreshing shower, not the dreary downpour I'd felt at the moment.

How many similar moments have I missed because I chose to wear the blinders of an inflexible agenda?

A new cloud, heavy with regret, settled on my heart, and I turned to my Bible for an attitude adjustment. It amazed me to discover that the underlying cause of my inflexibility is rooted in love—or in my case, an underdeveloped version of it. I believe God has been dealing with this flaw in me for a while. I've read the following verses plenty of times, but removing my blinders sheds fresh light on them:

> If I could speak [or write] all the languages of earth and of angels, but didn't love others, I would only be a noisy gong or a clanging cymbal. If I had the gift of prophecy, and if I understood all of God's secret plans and possessed all knowledge, and if I had such faith that I could move mountains, but didn't love others, I would be nothing... Love is patient and kind...It is not irritable, and it keeps no record of being wronged (1 Corinthians 13:1-2,4-5).

Upon reading this passage today, I saw myself on stage in a darkened theater. Suddenly, huge floodlights overhead shone directly on me. I squinted into the audience and saw rows of vacant seats.

Wait a minute. Vacant as in *empty?*

Yep.

No one was there to applaud the grand performance they were confident I'd pull off. All my running and doing and striving toward accomplishment—that agenda I'd clutched at and guarded frantically—for what? How often have I protected my time more than the well-being of loved ones who needed attention or strangers who needed a smile?

Now I'm experiencing glimpses of verses 11 and 12: "When I was a child, I spoke and thought and reasoned as a child. But when I grew up, I put away childish things. Now we see things imperfectly as in a cloudy mirror, but then we will see everything with perfect clarity."

Turns out I am really bad at loving. However, I do appear to be adept at fooling myself with a selfish version of it—that is, when I haven't been interrupted too many times. Obviously, lasting character change will require more than an internal epiphany.

In *The Letters of C. S. Lewis to Arthur Greeves,* Lewis wrote, "The great thing, if one can, is to stop regarding all the unpleasant things as interruptions of one's 'own' or 'real' life. The truth is of course that what one calls the interruptions are precisely one's real life—the life God is sending one day by day: what one calls one's 'real life' is a phantom of one's own imagination."

There is no such thing as *my* time if I truly want a life that God uses. I don't own my day; it's his. And time is nothing to him. He transcends it, and he can bring huge productivity out of a meager five minutes. When we allow him room to "mess" with our schedules, his time will always be enough.

Novelist Jane Kirkpatrick wrote that she often thinks her work is to write, when actually her work is "to engage, to be aware, to listen to God's calling." Love engages. It makes time. And it does it with a smile.

When we prioritize people over tasks we not only invite opportunities to encourage others, we also enrich our lives with deepened relationships and lifelong memories. Interruptions may actually be gifts that open us up to a world of possibility outside the narrow scope of our blinders.

God gave me such a gift today despite my impatient whining. All the while I was throwing an adult-sized tantrum, he was preparing my workday. He took my childishness and molded it into this writing, bringing the day to a unique completion only he could foresee. Might it be that I'm one hairsbreadth closer to appreciating an interruption, recognizing it as a divine gift?

Maybe I am growing just a little.

But what happens when we live God's way? He brings gifts into our lives, much the same way that fruit appears in an orchard—things like affection for

others, exuberance about life, serenity. We develop a
willingness to stick with things, a sense of compassion
in the heart, and a conviction that a basic holiness
permeates things and people. We find ourselves involved
in loyal commitments, not needing to force our way in
life, able to marshal and direct our energies wisely.

GALATIANS 5:22-23 MSG

CONSIDER THIS...

1. What drives your day? What motivates you to get up in the morning? Would you describe yourself as a driven person? What goals or ambitions are you driven to achieve?

2. How often do you find yourself frustrated by interruptions to your plans? What situations or people trigger those feelings? How do you typically respond?

3. Think back to a time when you chose your agenda over the needs of someone else. If you could redo your actions, would you do things differently? If so, how?

4. King Solomon was known for his wisdom. Toward the end of his life, he wrote the book of Ecclesiastes—his own set of hindsights as he reflected on the meaning of life. What do these verses tell you about how experience and years of living affect perspective? Ecclesiastes 2:22-24; 5:13-20; 9:11-12.

5. A gentle spirit is a rare treasure that the Bible frequently mentions. What insights do these verses offer about the effects of a quiet spirit or a gentle response? Ecclesiastes 10:4; Isaiah 32:17; Ephesians 4:1-3; Philippians 4:5; Colossians 3:12-13. How might gentleness and the Holy Spirit's peace influence a person's response to interruptions?

4

LOVE CAN TAKE YOUR BREATH AWAY, BUT TRUE LOVE GIVES YOU BIGGER LUNGS.

Take a deep breath. Energizing, isn't it? Or maybe it's relaxing. Either way, that oxygen is good stuff.

Okay, now my turn...Ahhh. Actually, I needed to breathe deeply because of this topic. It's a vulnerable one that's going to require some embarrassing admissions. But hey, growth is painful, so I'll suck it up and deal. Aren't I so strong?

Love. Romance. Heart-stopping glances and breathless kisses. Fun! We all long for love and yearn for the kind that fills up those cracks and crevices inside us that come from too much time alone. We need love like we need air. We're created for it by God, who calls himself love (1 John 4:8,16).

As we're all aware, love comes in many varieties. But since the romantic kind is often the most confusing and misunderstood, that's the one we'll focus on here.

As a teen and early twentysomething, I had some fairly mature attitudes about love. For starters, I was determined not to settle for someone I knew wasn't God's best choice for me. I had high expectations of marriage and was willing to wait until I knew that I knew that I knew God was handing me the match of his choice.

But in other ways—what a goober! Since I'm being all honest here,

I have to admit that I could be quite the love flake. In love with love. Head in the clouds. Dreamer to the extreme. I did myself no favors by putting guys I was interested in on pedestals no human could live up to. As a result, I scared myself out of really getting to know most of them. I also did myself no favors by dismissing some decent prospects because I wasn't crazy about their cars or their clothes or their whatever. You name it. I was a bubblehead.

God bless my husband.

I love my love story. Maybe I appreciate it all the more because it seemed so long in coming. But even if Steve and I had found each other years earlier, I'm certain I'd still be pretty crazy about him had I not had to wait for him. He's truly a gift, the best one God has given me besides salvation. Looking back, I can see how God's timing worked perfectly for us. We both had to grow in our individual ways in order to be ready for each other, and our relationship is stronger for it.

But the wait was not easy. In fact, it often was suffocating while I watched friends and siblings and cousins find their true loves and settle into marital bliss.

However, as he does so well, God used the waiting time to refine some of my mixed-up views and ways of processing emotions. And he taught me that the breathless love of my girlhood dreams simply wasn't enough. In love's waiting room, he did some major transplanting and gave me bigger lungs.

I mentioned that I love my love story. I should tell you that even as a young girl I wanted God to write my romance in a way that was undeniably his handwriting. I wanted the real thing, not the settled-for-probably-good-enough version. I wanted the Cinderella fairy tale only he could create.

He gave it to me.

Although Steve and I lived five hundred miles apart when we met as adults, we soon discovered our lives had crossed paths long before that. We grew up ten miles from each other, and our families attended the same small church for a while, which happens to be where we ended up getting married. (Let me hear that sigh...isn't it too sweet?) We remember several of the same families, can talk about locations and stores in the area, and still laugh whenever we see a lobster tank in a grocery store because it brings back similar memories of hanging out at the lobster tank in the old Dominick's on Schmale in Wheaton, Illinois.

But we didn't know all that until we met online some 20 years later. Yep, you read that right. We're one of *those* couples who fell in love over cyberspace. And you read the other part right too...our paths crossed as kids, only to be brought back together by God's miracle many years later. Is that a fairy tale or what?

There are many other "coincidences" I could relay, like friends at our separate colleges who knew us both and countless direct answers to prayer. But this really isn't about my love story, so let's get on with the topic at hand.

All of us have made and will continue to make mistakes in love, whether it's expecting someone else to make us whole or to fulfill all our needs or taking for granted that we deserve love. Here's the abbreviated truth: No one can, no one will, and we don't.

First of all, if we don't go into love as a healthy and whole person, then we only invite strife and heartache by hoping another human will complete us. None of us is wired to carry that kind of burden; it's enough to keep our own junk together without being expected to fix someone else's. Even though love is powerful and can bring healing, human love is flawed.

As for expecting someone to fulfill all our needs? Come on, let's be realistic. Have *you* ever been able to do that for someone? Would you ever be so audacious to think you could?

Again, not our job.

Finally, the idea that we deserve love. This one's tricky, and we may not like the answer. But the truth is, from God's holy perspective—going directly to the top for this one—we're fortunate recipients of his perfect love, not entitled to it in our own right. It's only because of Jesus' death on our behalf that God even considers inviting us into a relationship with him.

Before you hurl this book across the room, let me say it sounds harsh to my humanness too. After all, I'm a mostly decent person. At least I think I am, despite my generous portion of faults. But from God's viewpoint, that opinion just reveals my incomplete understanding of holiness and purity versus deficient human nature.

I know God loves me more than I can fathom, but the reality is, he doesn't have to give me a passing glance. He's God. I'm only human. I'm one blessed cookie to have been saved by his grace, and not only saved, but cherished, delighted in, prized, and cradled in his care. But the fact remains that if Jesus had not died to pay for my innate sinfulness—which I can do nothing on my own to overcome—God could not look at me with love-filled eyes. He's holy, and holiness cannot mix with imperfection. We may not like it, but it's right there in the Bible:

> You know the story of how Adam landed us in the dilemma we're in—first sin, then death, and no one exempt from either sin or death. That sin disturbed relations with God in everything and everyone…So death, this huge abyss separating us from God, dominated the landscape…Even those who didn't sin precisely as Adam did by disobeying a specific command of God still had to experience this termination of life, this separation from God (Romans 5:12-14 MSG).

So we don't deserve God's kind of love, the real kind. Where does that leave us, and what does it have to do with our relationships?

Let's get back to the mistakes we make in love. One of the most widespread love blunders has to do with our lung capacity. We long for the breathless excitement of romance and fool ourselves by thinking it couldn't get any better than that. However, there's a problem with that kind.

What happens when you're out of breath? You gasp and wheeze

and act in desperation to take in air. When someone is suffocating, every thought, every instinct is pointed toward survival. Everything becomes all about that person's needs.

Going into a romantic relationship with that kind of personal emptiness is not what the Great Phys Ed Trainer ordered. It fools us into thinking that our role in a love relationship is to get filled, which goes back to our messed-up view that we deserve it.

God is a marathon runner when it comes to love. He set for us an example of a giving love, not a selfish kind that leaves us struggling to get our own needs met. Without his love, we'd all be dying—and not just in this lifetime, but for eternity. With a crucial *but,* he pumped spiritual oxygen into us in the midst of our final gasps for air: "But God showed his great love for us by sending Christ to die for us while we were still sinners" (Romans 5:8). That kind of giving comes only from God-sized love lungs.

God gave us his Son Jesus, not out of a need to earn our love, but because his own perfect love longed to overflow into us. He's got some incredible lung capacity to be able to spare that kind of love and still be perfectly whole and holy.

There's no getting around it: We're loveable only because he loves us. Not only that, but we are capable of his kind of love only because he empowers us by stretching and training and enlarging our love lungs to handle such a workout. First John 4:19 says so: "We love each other because he loved us first," or as another version succinctly puts it, "First we were loved, now we love" (MSG). Since our ability to love—our love-lung capacity—depends on our knowing his love first, it goes without saying that the *quality* of our love directly relates to the depth of his love that we experience.

When we gain firsthand understanding of the power of his love, we are changed from the inside. God's love heals, restores, soothes, refreshes, and repairs those cracks we all have inside, and we become whole individuals. Our lungs expand and become capable of taking in an abundance of air, and we can't help wanting to share the overflow with others.

We become givers.

Hosea was such a giver. He's the guy God told to marry a prostitute. Now, a past is a past, and grace is huge enough to cover anything. But Hosea's one and only hadn't given up her career, and she wasn't about to anytime soon after the wedding. God was telling Hosea to take on guaranteed heartache. So much for dreams of finding a perfect human love. Hosea was looking at years of being the giver, of showing unselfish devotion to someone who would stomp on his heart and then toss it out with the trash. Repeatedly.

Of course, God had an important reason for putting this burden on Hosea. He was creating a picture of Israel's spiritual unfaithfulness to him. Hosea's unwavering faithfulness to his wife, Gomer, would illustrate God's true love for us. God said of Israel, "I will make you my wife forever, showing you righteousness and justice, unfailing love and compassion...I will show love to those I called 'Not loved'" (Hosea 2:19,23).

How could Hosea do it? It's a double whammy. First, he had to give up his dreams of being loved, of having a solid marriage. Then he had to give and give to someone who, as far as he knew, would never put even half the effort into making their relationship work.

The only way anyone could have endured that kind of drain is by drawing on God for vitality. By deepening our relationship with God, we receive the refreshing air of his love. Hosea 6:3 says, "Oh, that we might know the Lord! Let us press on to know him. He will respond to us as surely as the arrival of dawn or the coming of rains in early spring."

Learning to love takes a lifetime, and it's not for the spiritually asthmatic. I often wondered why I wasn't ready earlier for my true love. The truth was, I needed to make God my truer love first. I thought he was, but it took years of training to help me wake up to a few crucial realities about being satisfied in Christ. He stretched my endurance because he knew I could have the marriage I longed for only when I found my wholeness in a relationship with him.

Now, a few years into marriage, I'm discovering still more areas of *me* that crowd out *him*. For the rest of my life, God will gradually expand my ability to love more fully.

God had reasons for choosing Gomer for Hosea, just as he has reasons for the path of my love story and yours. But his overarching goal for each of us will always be for us to know his love more deeply so we can love him and others more purely.

In order to run the marathon of lifelong love, let your spiritual Physician, Trainer, and Coach equip you with endurance and the refreshment of his love. Breathe deeply of that love, and let him expand your love-lung capacity. Determine to become the kind of lover—romantic and otherwise—who can handle the rigorous workout that truly loving someone else demands.

Don't settle for loving breathlessly. Go for the bigger lungs. They're yours if you're willing to stick with God's training plan.

I pray that from his glorious, unlimited resources he will empower you with inner strength through his Spirit...Your roots will grow down into God's love and keep you strong. And may you have the power to understand, as all God's people should, how wide, how long, how high, and how deep his love is. May you experience the love of Christ, though it is too great to understand fully. Then you will be made complete with all the fullness of life and power that comes from God.

EPHESIANS 3:16-19

CONSIDER THIS...

1. How have your views on love and romance changed in the past five years? Ten years? What qualities about you serve as strengths in a love relationship? What areas need stretching so your love-lung capacity can grow?

2. Who or what has influenced your views on romantic love? How would you summarize your personal experience of God's love for you? How has your perception of his love affected your experience of human love, for good or bad? Does it give you peace or test your faith to trust God to write your human love story, whether it's in progress, yet to come, or not in his plan for you? How might you address this with him if it tests your faith more than it brings you peace?

3. Jesus said God's greatest command is to love him, followed by his second command to love others (Matthew 22:37-39). How does the rest of life fall into place when these two command-ments are followed well? What does a relationship look like when both people live them out? How can one person's obedience to these commands positively impact a relationship even if the other person does not follow them?

4. First Corinthians 13 is known as the love chapter. Verses 1-3 list qualities that might fake us into thinking we're doing life well, even if we might not be so great at loving. How have you been fooled by your own tendency to substitute other performance abil-ities (such as having faith or giving gifts or acquiring knowledge) as opposed to showing true love for others? Which qualities of love as listed in verses 4-7 have you struggled with? Which do you appreciate most as gifts from others to you? From God to you?

5. Read through Galatians 5:13–6:10, including the list of the fruit of the Spirit in Galatians 5:22-23. Those qualities go hand in hand with what 1 Corinthians 13 says about love, because all the qualities listed in both those chapters require a spiritual work of God before they'll become part of our makeup. Which fruit of the Spirit do you need to work on most? Which ones does your personality need most from others? (Gut-level honesty needed here!) Now focus on Galatians 5:13. How does the idea of spiritual freedom tie into our love-lung capacity and how freely we breathe God's love to others?

5

DREAMS WORTH CHASING ARE WORTH A LONG-DISTANCE RUN.

I love to run. Well, let me temper that: I *like* to *jog*. A real runner would know the difference.

Even though I enjoy jogging, I am not a born runner. In fact, I struggled through childhood right on up to my late twenties to jog more than a city block. Don't get me wrong, I could keep up with most people doing many other forms of exercise. Heart was good, flexibility above average, strength adequate. I didn't even hate the idea of working out. I enjoyed aerobics, dance, power walking, tennis, biking, hiking, you name it. But there was something about running that taxed my lungs to the point that I felt defeated even thinking about it.

When I was around 20, a doctor finally diagnosed me with sports asthma. At last I had a genuine reason, or at least a valid excuse, for the strange phenomenon I had come to think of as my running phobia. I had no big dreams of running a marathon, but my competitive nature had never wanted to accept that I couldn't run. I'm no wuss; I just hadn't developed the get-up-and-go to push past the hurdle I'd always believed was at least half mental instead of all physical.

And then one year I bought an elliptical machine. Consistent effort on that strengthened my lungs and gave me a close taste of the runner's high I'd heard so much about. Oh my, that high is worth the discipline. One year later, there I was jogging three miles on a treadmill. Turns out, what I needed was some endurance training and a stick-to-it attitude.

My little dream of being a jogger may not seem like much to you, but I know the subtle feeling that nagged me all my life until I accomplished my goal. It was the feeling that there was something more, something bigger I'd been resigned to living without. For the past bunch of years since exercise has become a lifestyle, I have enjoyed this success. It's been a boost to my confidence as well as to my all-around health.

And perhaps even more important, it's become a daily reminder that dreams, no matter how big or small, are worth going the distance to achieve.

You may have noticed the recent trend toward TV reality shows. You've probably seen at least one or two dozen. If I never watch another one I'll live a completely fulfilled life.

However, as weary of them as I have become, one in particular has caught my attention. Have you seen *The Biggest Loser*? The determination and commitment those contestants exhibit is truly inspiring to anyone who's ever dreamed of anything.

I know how tough it still is at times to get out of bed in the wee morning hours to work out. Well, that show puts me to shame. Not only do the contestants battle each pound, step, and food decision—plus the separation from loved ones—they also must fight demons of negativity as they strive for a distant goal they don't know if they can come close to achieving.

After training for weeks to establish their path toward success, they're sent home and test their dedication on their own. Cut loose from the security and support of their trainers and fellow competitors, each person must prove how much their dream means.

And then the finale. *Amazing.*

You'd never guess many of the contestants are the same people in the photos of their former selves. Working off an excess of one or even two hundred pounds drops more than just body weight. It drops any doubt about the worth of going after a goal.

Their faces come alive with the life change they've accomplished. By refusing their doubts, self-condemnation, and defeatist mentalities—things we all struggle with in our own unique battles—they gain a knowledge they'll thrive on the rest of their lives. They have a firsthand knowledge of pushing toward a dream and not giving up, of never again settling for giving less than their best in any area of life.

Have you stopped to think about God's dreams for you? He is the ultimate Dreamer. None of us dreams big enough compared to God's desires for us. I believe many people have developed skewed concepts of what it means to dream. Tragic.

To my thinking, there are several pitfalls to the realization of a dream.

First of all, some people are raised or trained to believe that dreams are a waste of time. Impractical, irresponsible fantasies that get in the way of real grown-up living. These dream-suffocators end up frustrated and cynical from the disappointments that rankle their lives. Life continues to let them down because they have shut out the deeper call God has been whispering to their hearts.

Well, pish posh on that load of...

Anyway. On to the second pitfall. In this second category sit those who have never even learned *how* to dream for themselves. They aren't against dreams. They watch and admire other people who show the guts to pursue their heart's desires, but it never sinks in that God may have more for them as well. Great things happen to other people, not to them. These folks may be hard workers, or their sofa cushions may be imprinted with impressions of their backsides. Either way, there's room for enrichment in the lives of these nondreamers.

Third, there are the dream-wasters. This lazy bunch definitely needs to replace their couches. Big dips in the cushions from too much sitting around with heads in the clouds. They spend so much time living in Dreamland that they don't emerge long enough to do what's necessary to make those dreams part of their reality.

And, finally, the dream-demanders. Similar in some ways to the dream-wasters, people who fall into this fourth category are so wrapped up in what *could* be that they miss out on what *is*. They're not lazy, though. Instead, they're overly focused to the detriment of a balanced life. As a result, they forego perks of current life along the way to achieving their goals. Their self-inflicted demands rob them of time to connect with God, family, and friends, as well as for rebuilding energy and maintaining a healthy perspective. Their attention is so wrapped up in themselves that their dream becomes a source of negativity.

So here's the expected question: Do you fit in any of those categories?

Hope not.

While we're on the subject, what are your attitudes toward your dreams? Do you know the heart's burn that comes from a dream planted by God?

Hope so.

We've run through some negative approaches to dreams. Time to look more closely at God's view. Just what are his intentions for creating us with unique dreams?

He's a visionary as well as a doer, so certainly his plans for us are purposeful. However, his primary goal for us is not our personal fulfillment. That would contradict his number one priority to bring glory to himself and his number one command that we're supposed to love him above all else, including our dreams (Deuteronomy 6:5; Matthew 22:36-38).

Psalm 37:4 says, "Delight yourself in the LORD and he will give you the desires of your heart" (NIV). That verse typically is taken to mean that when we put God first, he will give us the things we desire most.

But it could also mean that when we seek God's will for our lives, he straightens out our dreams and plants within us ("gives us") certain goals. In other words, our desire for him above everything else creates and directs the dreams that become most important to us. He leads us to the fulfillment of them and actually uses them to deepen our relationship with him. Loving God first changes us from the inside, so naturally we might expect that our dreams could morph as we come to know God more intimately.

See the difference?

One thing we can be sure of is that his purposes for our dreams go far beyond their role in our lives. We will stifle our success when we're primarily in it for selfish reasons. When we make gods of our dreams, our one true God cannot and will not bless them with lasting success. In fact, sometimes God uses our dreams to test our willingness to put him first.

Take a look at Deuteronomy 13:1-4 (MSG) for more on this:

> When a prophet or visionary…says, "Let's follow other gods…let's worship them," don't pay any attention to what that prophet or visionary says. God, your God, is testing you to find out if you totally love him with everything you have in you. You are to follow only God, your God, hold him in deep reverence, keep his commandments, listen obediently to what he says, serve him—hold on to him for dear life!

When you put your hopes in God's hands and make him your focus, he'll line up your dreams with his. And he'll lead you on the adventure of a lifetime, directly related to his best interests for you.

But you've got to be ready for the ups and downs of the adventure. It'll be like nothing you could prepare for on your own. God-things usually aren't. That's why they're God-things. Again, he wants to expand our experience of him through the desires he plants in us. When he takes us to our limits, we're in for an exciting view of him at work.

I read recently in Exodus about the Israelites' journey out of Egyptian slavery. For so long they envisioned freedom, yearned for a better life, for the *more* they'd begged of God. Finally, he issued the "On your mark, get set, go!" call to Moses, their reluctant leader.

At last their dreams were coming true. You'd think they'd be all aflutter with excitement as each step carried them farther from the confinements of their past. It didn't take long, however, for fear to kick in. One view of the first obstacle had them plagued with doubts and complaints.

Like many of us, they apparently wanted a smooth road to the prize.

Take a quick look at Exodus 14:10-12:

> As Pharaoh approached, the people of Israel looked up and panicked when they saw the Egyptians overtaking them. They cried out to the LORD, and they said to Moses, "Why did you bring us out here to die in the wilderness? Weren't there enough graves for us in Egypt? What have you done to us? Why did you make us leave Egypt? Didn't we tell you this would happen while we were still in Egypt? We said, 'Leave us alone! Let us be slaves to the Egyptians. It's better to be a slave in Egypt than a corpse in the wilderness!' "

The gripes! The groans! The drama! Don't you want to tell them to quit bellyaching already?

Yet how many of us fall into the same shortsighted snare, the one that fools us into thinking that remaining enslaved to a stationary life is preferable to God's adventure?

Ugh. Lord, don't let us settle for so little.

In *He Still Moves Stones,* Max Lucado writes,

> There is a rawness and a wonder to life. Pursue it. Hunt for it. Sell out to get it. Don't listen to the whines of those who have settled for a second-rate life and want you to do the same so they won't feel guilty. Your goal is not to live long; it's to live.
>
> Jesus says the options are clear. On one side there is the

voice of safety. You can build a fire in the hearth, stay inside, and stay warm and dry and safe. You can't get hurt if you never get out, right? You can't be criticized for what you don't try, right? You can't fall if you don't take a stand, right? You can't lose your balance if you never climb, right? So don't try it. Take the safe route. Or you can hear the voice of adventure—God's adventure. Instead of building a fire in your hearth, build a fire in your heart. Follow God's impulses. Adopt the child. Move overseas. Teach the class. Change careers. Run for office. Make a difference. Sure it isn't safe, but what is?[1]

It's a mistake to choose "safety" over the adventure of following God's impulse. We show our ignorance when we view any place as safer than smack-dab in the center of God's design for us.

Powerful for good or bad, dreams can launch us toward success, or they can push the imprint of our backside deeper in the sofa cushion if we've come to view those dreams as impossible, impractical, not worthwhile, or if we haven't committed them to God.

Far from being silly wastes of time, dreams are crucial birthplaces for fulfillment—at least the ones planted in us by God. And the best ones require a whole-being commitment that refuses to give up.

As for the goal that's been kicking around your brain while you've read this? Absolutely, it could require marathon effort to reach it. It could take you to the edge of your faith and demand more gumption than you've ever had to lay hold of. In all likelihood it will. But never underestimate the prize of seeing it come true. If you've heard God's *On your mark!* call, are you listening closely for the upcoming *Get set?* And are you ready to *Go* when the starter pistol fires?

You and God. You're quite a match for accomplishing great things together. Get alone with him and submit to his training program. He knows exactly how to prepare you for the changing terrain. Above all, he wants you to know him better along the course to your dreams.

Don't resign yourself to a life that lacks the more God wants for you. You've got one run on this earth. Go the distance with him for your shared dreams, and discover the gorgeous view at the finish line.

God can do anything, you know—far more than you could ever imagine or guess or request in your wildest dreams! He does it not by pushing us around but by working within us, his Spirit deeply and gently within us.

EPHESIANS 3:20 MSG

CONSIDER THIS...

1. Dream with me for a few minutes. In your ideal imaginings, what does your life look like five years from now? Ten? Twenty? Thirty? If time and money weren't issues, what would you like to do that you aren't currently doing? Do you have a plan of action? What might you have to sacrifice or let go of in order to achieve your dream? To what level have you committed this goal to God?

2. What are your greatest dream-busters? Are those attackers based within you, or do they come from outside sources? What strategies have you developed to combat them? In weak moments, which of the four categories of dream pitfalls pulls you down (dream-suffocators, nondreamers, dream-wasters, dream-demanders)? What emotions rise to the surface when you imagine your dream coming true?

3. Take a close look at Philippians 3:12-15. These verses talk about focusing, pressing on, putting the past behind, looking forward to what lies ahead, and striving for a heavenly prize. How does each of those efforts tie into a particular dream you hold? Verse 15

also mentions spiritual maturity. How does your current depth of spiritual maturity influence how you view your dreams?

4. First Corinthians 9:24-25 speaks of running to win, and of a Christian's ultimate goal in eternity. How would you define God's goals for you, in your own words? How well do your current dreams fit with God's highest goals for you? If you've known God for any length of time, can you recognize areas he has changed in you? Do you see a need to stretch your dreams to be more in line with God's purposes for you?

5. It's common to face doubts about the worth of our dreams as well as our abilities to achieve them. How do the following verses encourage you to partner more closely with God as you pursue your goals? Psalm 19:14; Proverbs 10:28; 16:9; Jeremiah 29:11-13; Philippians 4:13. How do the following verses about God fulfilling people's desires in the past encourage you in your doubts? First Samuel 1:1-20; Luke 1:36-37; 2:25-38.

6

WANT THE PLAN?
READ THE BLUEPRINT.

I ran my fingers over the surface of the bookcase and wondered what titles would fill the shelves. A piece this size could hold a couple hundred books. I picked up the paint brush and wrinkled my nose at the fumes. One more coat of polyurethane ought to do it. Though glad to have this job, I'd be glad to finish all the same. I lifted my face to the Mexican autumn sun. At least we'd been able to set up my workstation outside the workshop, where a breeze dispersed the odor. With careful strokes, I began the finishing coat. One of two, this handcrafted bookcase would serve the church well. The guys were doing a great job.

Speaking of them, I listened to their laughter mix with the buzz of power tools inside the shop as they fashioned more furniture for the sanctuary and offices. Bookshelves, risers, plant stands, flag holders…items our team had been asked to build during our week helping this church in Puebla, Mexico.

Our mission team had been split into several groups, and Steve and I were part of the construction crew. With his background in building, he'd been chosen as one of the skilled workers to craft those pieces. As his wife, I was a shoo-in for polyurethane duty.

Across the lawn, a tent hummed with activity from the medical crews and their patients. Dozens of local residents filled chairs in a makeshift waiting area, while nurses, doctors, dentists, and various other team members administered free health care to the impoverished community.

I was excited to be here on this mission trip with Steve. So much of normal life revolved around ourselves at home; it felt good to focus outside our everyday zone.

I sensed we were part of something bigger, and I couldn't help thinking back to the Bible study I'd done the previous summer about the Old Testament tabernacle. God had specific guidelines for constructing each aspect of his house, and he handpicked skilled workers for that all-important assignment (Exodus 35–40).

Now, many centuries later, Steve was another one of those pros, selected to do nothing less than a stellar job on the furnishings for the Lord's house. And I got to have a close-up part in it too.

The connection between the first worship structure and this one struck me on a wave of fumes.

With the sun shining overhead and sounds of hope floating over the yard, I knew I was experiencing another never-forget-it moment.

My husband and I have very different offices. A recent visit to his reminded me how foreign his work language is to me. Although I'm worlds of information ahead of where I was when we met—hey, I know what rebar is, and I know to frown on construction sites that neglect a vapor barrier or the hazards of rainfall before a structure is roofed in—I still have a lot to learn about the complexities of a set of blueprints.

Steve, in contrast, has been a construction project manager for more than a dozen years. The language is as familiar to him as my writing style manuals are to me. He can envision an entire building just by looking at the blueprints. It boggles my mind how he pictures the whole image from a bunch of scrawled lines and tiny measurements, but he can see beyond the sketches to the intended design.

He's got skills, I tell ya. Skills that took years of training and even more practice. I suppose I shouldn't be too hard on myself for being ignorant when it comes to understanding blueprints. After all, I've spent my years honing English skills, not construction management ones.

It occurred to me on that memorable day in Puebla, Mexico, that understanding the Bible takes training and practice as well. Maybe staring at the bookshelves brought it on, wondering what volumes of biblical reference would line them, imagining the pastor studying some element of doctrine to share with his congregation.

I love the Bible. Love it, love it, love it.

I can't say that's always been the case. I never had terrible feelings about it, but for years it seemed nothing more than a hefty stack of tissue-thin paper filled with confusing stories and old-fashioned rules bound together by many different cover materials. Now you can find Bibles in metal covers, on cassettes, DVDs, and CDs. You can find entire Bible texts online in a wide range of translations. There are Bibles available for every group imaginable. Bibles for women, for men, for teens, for children, for babies. And more for couples, singles, seniors, and professionals. Bibles in countless languages, all saying the same thing in ways fitted for many nationalities.

Growing up, we had lots of Bibles in our house. I've probably had at least 20 of my own. But I never appreciated the sacredness of that book until life drove me to search its depths for what I knew I was missing. And now I cannot imagine life without it.

I *love* the Bible.

I love that God wrote it for me. Okay, he wrote it for all of us, but he also wrote it for *each* of us. It's not just a group message; it's intimately individual. This may sound clichéd, but the Bible is the Maker and Savior of the Universe's love letter to each person he ever created.

So heads up. That means you.

How's your comprehension of God's Word? Do you get that its message is for your every need? If not, you're missing out on the best gift. The Bible's good stuff—vital stuff. But it does take conscientious effort to understand how deep it goes.

I think God did this on purpose. Actually, I know he did because the Bible itself says so. Look at Joshua 1:8: "Study this Book of Instruction continually. Meditate on it day and night so you will be sure to obey everything written in it. Only then will you prosper and succeed in all you do."

Our understanding of the Bible is directly related to our efforts. Of course, we need God's spiritual power to help us get it (John 14:16-17, 25-26), but we do have a part in our own biblical education.

That's not to say it requires professional degrees to understand the story of his love. It actually takes a simple heart. See what Luke 10:21-22 (CEV) says:

> At that same time, Jesus felt the joy that comes from the Holy Spirit, and he said: My Father, Lord of heaven and earth, I am grateful that you hid all this from wise and educated people and showed it to ordinary people. Yes, Father, that is what pleased you. My Father has given me everything, and he is the only one who knows the Son. The only one who really knows the Father is the Son. But the Son wants to tell others about the Father, so that they can know him too.

I love the fact that God, who could have made things more complex than any human could handle, chose to communicate at an ordinary person's level. Other translations say God reveals it to the "childlike" (NLT), the "newcomers" (MSG), the "childish, unskilled, and untaught" (AMP). That pretty much opens it up to everyone, except those who think they're wise enough on their own.

The Bible is like blueprints for knowing God and building a relationship with him. Just as it takes training, time, and practice to learn the ins and outs of construction blueprints, seeing the deeper things in God's Word requires those disciplines as well.

Scripture is loaded with symbolism relating to foundations, construction, and counting the cost in relation to life. Psalm 24:2, for example: "[The LORD] laid the earth's foundation on the seas and built it on the ocean depths." Isaiah even prophesied about Jesus the Messiah, calling him a foundation stone (Isaiah 28:16).

How appropriate that Jesus was a carpenter by trade. Not only is he the firm foundation, but he's well aware from personal experience what it means to build a relationship with his heavenly Father.

An accurate set of blueprints shows how to construct a sturdy building with a firm foundation. Similarly, a successful life is not just born, it is built. It requires knowing the Carpenter's plans as they're revealed in his Blueprint for life.

The Bible is an ever-ready conversation with the Lord. If we'd carve out time each day to learn his language, we'd be overwhelmed by how close he is to us in those tissue-thin pages. We'll also understand what he wants to do in our lives.

But we have to want it.

I learned to want him in my early twenties, when life felt very uncertain. It's always at my lowest points, feeling like the ground could crumble at any moment, when I'm drawn to God's Word the most. That's when I replant my feet on his solid foundation that never shifts under me.

When we spend time learning God's messages to us, we spare ourselves much anxiety because we're able to call to mind his promises, we're able to combat Satan's attacks with truth, and we keep building our connection with God. We also are well trained to take part in a much bigger project he's been working on since he first laid the foundations of the earth.

He is already in the process of building his Church, which includes everyone who has followed him for all time. He sent his Son, the Carpenter, to invite us to be a part of this foundation. The most skilled workers are those who invest in training to understand the language of his work. They'll be best equipped to help with the construction.

God doesn't want shoddy workmanship when it comes to his people. Those who are trained by the ultimate Construction Manager ought to know their stuff. They ought to be capable of capturing his vision for the big eternal picture. And they ought to be willing to put in a good life's work. First Corinthians 3:10-13 (MSG) says,

> Let each carpenter who comes on the job take care to build on the foundation! Remember there is only one foundation, the one already laid: Jesus Christ. Take particular care in picking out your building materials. Eventually there is going to be an inspection. If you use cheap or inferior materials, you'll be found out.

I felt lost in Mexico when I couldn't communicate with the locals in their language because I'd never taken the time to learn it. How much more lost do we feel when we try to do life without knowing the language of the Builder of life? He has a special language with each of his children, a heart's connection between his and yours.

He's ready and able to develop that connection with you, and he offers his Blueprint so you have a clue to his ways. He has plans for building your life along with you, but you've got to know the Blueprint. In order to know that, you've got to learn his language. The only way to accomplish that is to pore over his Word.

Your faith in him is one building project guaranteed to weather the storms of life in direct proportion to the effort you put into its construction.

This life is the only one you have, so take care to build well.

Dear friends, keep building on the foundation of your most holy faith, as the Holy Spirit helps you to pray.

JUDE 1:20 CEV

CONSIDER THIS...

1. Have there been times when you've sensed God speaking to you? What were the circumstances? How did this affect you, and what was your response? What Scriptures, if any, have spoken powerfully to you? Why?

2. To what extent have you taken an active role in building God's kingdom (his church)? Is this something that interests you? If not, what holds you back? Are you willing to commit to search his Word in order to know him better?

3. First Peter 2:1-8 connects our growth as Christians (verses 1-3) with Jesus as the cornerstone (verses 4-8). Verses 1-3 say that we mature in our faith because we examine and see how good Jesus is. How has your faith matured as you've experienced God at work in your life? What part can you play in continuing to grow your faith?

4. The book of Job describes a conversation between Job and God when Job grieves for the wreck of his life. God sets him straight with a bunch of questions, some of which remind Job (and us) just who we're dealing with. God is the ultimate Constructor. What does Hebrews 3:4 say to you about who is building your life? Do you view him as your life builder? How does the vision that God is growing you impact your pursuit of him?

5. Not only is Jesus the firm foundation, but he is well aware from personal experience the high construction costs of living in obedience to his Father. Read Luke 14:25-30 about counting the cost of living as a strong Christian. What sacrifices might you have to make (or have made already) to live for him?

7

GET SURE-FOOTED IN YOUR OWN SHOES.

Our first Mini-Marshall is baking away warm and cozy inside me as I type. Yep, we're pregnant.

As we settle further into the land of Surreal and our home fills with all things baby, I don't know which to be more awestruck by: the amount of gear we're told we need…or the size of the baby socks.

Have you ever looked at a newborn's sock? I'm telling you, there isn't anything cuter in all the land. My husband's thumb fills one up.

Okay, so maybe I exaggerate a bit. Not about the socks or the thumb, but about what moves me at having a little one on the way. I am flabbergasted at the prospect of raising a child. The fact that *I'm the mommy.* Anyone who has a baby without feeling a measure of intimidation is going into it blindly, I think.

If this child knew the power he or she has over me, surely a pint-sized sin nature would kick in and a pint-sized brain would find all manner of ways to work my emotions. To have Mom wrapped around that little finger from day one—oh, the possibilities!

The other day I told Steve that I'm scared of our baby. What frightens me is my long list of character flaws and weaknesses that leave me feeling insecure about myself. I'm scared that my humanness will wreck the perfect design God is forming, this individual soul Jesus died to save and loves even more than I do. I've actually been praying God's protection on this baby against inheriting my insecurities.

I'm scared of not being enough.

Parenting is a God-sized task with God-sized shoes to fill. Frankly, I am not enough. But then again, no parent is. Thankfully, God is plenty big to fill his own shoes, and he's ready to help us fill the shoes he gives us and to fit them for walking the path he leads us on.

Somehow in his graciousness, God picked me to be the mother for this new person. And somehow by his grace, I will become more sure-footed in my mothering shoes as I learn to approach each day in his strength. My mind knows God will help me be enough, but getting my heart to fully believe it is a more involved process.

As the weeks speed closer to the big day and I continue to become more well-rounded physically, I've been pondering what it means to be a well-rounded, self-assured person in all areas of life. My thoughts venture more often through my past and the challenges I faced while learning to accept myself as God created me. Some of my insecurities come from within, but others are a direct result of spoken and unspoken feedback from other people. We've all felt the sting of an insult or a derogatory look, and most of us have had to deal with some sort of blow to our reputation. How do we maintain a healthy self-image and live comfortably in our own shoes when the rest of the world seems bent on pointing out our trouble spots?

I've always had plenty of insecurities. It makes me laugh now, but some of my earliest memories of not being good enough stemmed from my height. I'm short; always have been. While it's a trait I'm fine with as an adult, in elementary school I took it for granted that my opinions didn't matter as much as the taller kid's. Typing that just now, I'm hit with how nutty our insecurities can be. But really, think what that belief would do to a kid on a daily basis.

And then there was my quietness. How I hated that word! If I had a penny for every time someone told me I was "*so* quiet"—even beyond my college years—well, I'd have that million to hire the house cleaner I've wanted!

Fortunately, age and maturity have proven kind in developing a healthier self-esteem. I suppose life has also given me a dose of cynicism that covers, even if it doesn't heal, emotional scar tissue from times when I didn't feel as though I measured up.

However, I'd still like to spare my child some growing-up angst at an earlier age. But how do I do that? People are not always kind. There's no way I can shield my little one from every hurt and insult. I want to help this tiny human know his or her intrinsic value and avoid being crushed emotionally by someone else's attacks on their personhood. How do I help solidify his or her identity despite conflicting feedback from others?

The answer is more involved than age and maturity and cynicism—but at the same time, it's really quite simple.

For better or worse, our early experiences in the big world often leave us doubtful about our identities, causing us to question our worth. The world is full of people who are full of opinions about us, whether we ask for them or not, regardless of their accuracy.

How I ever got the idea that my worth depended to any degree on my height I'll never know, but somewhere along the way that view planted itself and grew. It's a minor example of how impressionable we are and the upward battle we face to become healthy adults.

It took a long time for me to get comfortable in my shoes. Looking back, I can see more clearly the reasons for my identity struggles. They're pretty typical of most people.

In a nutshell, we are comfortable with ourselves only as deep as we go in our relationship with God.

Indulge me while I expand on this.

As a child, I could recite Bible verses about God's love. I knew in theory that he loved me and made me exactly as he knew best. The problem was, I didn't fully agree with his definition of best. I wanted to decide for him how I should have been made. I wished away my shyness, envying friends who could chat up a room at a party or flirt with unapologetic confidence.

As a result, I spent years missing out on some of God's best for me because I continued to let my insecurities trip me up. Sure, I was confident in some ways, but there were regions of my soul that needed to accept God's acceptance of me.

I love that: accepting God's acceptance of us. Packs a lot of simple truth, don't you think? Our struggle for identity isn't about God's view of us; it's about our view of God's view of us. God's very sure about his view. He never second-guesses how he makes anyone. When someone accepts that God has a perfect plan for them, they have the inner strength to move beyond criticism and enjoy living out their true potential.

Think through the people you know. Wide variety of confidence levels, right? Well, if you look harder at any one of those people, you're sure to notice fissures in their self-assurance. No one's self-esteem is completely solid, no matter how well they've learned to hide their insecurities.

Why? Because *self*-assurance is meager assurance. Insults, judgments, and critical feedback from others are like stones that get lodged in our shoes. Eventually they wear us down and leave us feeling raw. With enough wear and tear, over time we can end up feeling crippled in our attempts at doing life to our best ability. Some people compensate by building calluses over the hurt parts, like impenetrable shields that keep out more hurt. But those calluses also block out the potential for good emotions.

Without an identity rooted in the One who created us, it's impossible to have a whole self-esteem or to withstand harsh criticism and come out unscathed, much less better for it. In order to walk above the rocky road our reputations face, our confidence must come from belonging to God. When we're his, all other concerns of life fall into proper perspective.

I gained fresh perspective on these ideas recently. It's winter as I'm writing this. Christmas wasn't too long ago. During the holiday season I had a brainstorm about Mary, Jesus' mother. If anyone needed to rely on God-assurance rather than self-assurance, she did.

I'd never thought about the long-lasting effects of Mary becoming pregnant before she and Joseph were married. Surely there were plenty of folks—family, friends, neighbors, peers—who never bought her story. Not when she broke the news and not years later.

A pregnant virgin? The average Joe who heard the news would have walked away with a brief "Nuh-uh. Don't think so."

Really, let's be honest. Wouldn't you have been tempted to raise an eyebrow at that tale? As much as I love a good miracle, I would have questioned Mary's word.

Let's be honest as well about how shaken we would have been in her position. What would people think? And how in the world would she ever be enough to raise God's Son?

As far as we know, Mary had lived pure and wholesome, a girl to make any Israelite religious leader proud. Back then the sin she could have been wrongfully accused of was punishable by death (Deuteronomy 22:13-24), a threat powerful enough to leave anyone shaking in her shoes. And this girl was *young* when she first faced the onslaught to her reputation. The rumors likely lived on far beyond her lifetime. Lots of reason to feel very insecure in the shoes the Lord fitted for her. So how'd she stand up to the pressure?

If she had turned inward and given in to insecurities, or if she had built up calluses over her heart, there's no way she could have withstood the scandal with the grace she showed. The Bible acknowledges her tender human emotions. Luke 1:29 says she was "deeply troubled" (HCSB) or "thoroughly shaken" (MSG) by the angel's greeting. Naturally, she was as confused as anyone at the news that defied the birds and the bees. In modern English, her question might have gone very respectfully like this: "Um...well, Angel Gabe, there's this little problem called sex. I've never had it. How can I be pregnant?" (verse 34).

She felt the insecurity. She asked the question.

Then she immediately focused her mind on her God instead of on her uncertain road ahead or the attack her reputation would face.

Her next words the Bible records reveal a couple of vital qualities about Mary: "Oh, how my soul praises the Lord. How my spirit rejoices in God my Savior! For he took notice of his lowly servant girl, and from now on all generations will call me blessed" (verses 46-48).

First of all, they show where she found her assurance. She called herself lowly, but she didn't seem to use the word in a woe-is-me-I'm-dirt mentality. She merely saw her identity as lowly on her own merits. But she found joy and confidence in God's notice of her. He saw her as she was—no frills, no masks over her insecurities. And she accepted his acceptance of her.

Second, her words show how a God-view lifts us above the rocky road of our insecurities. There's no telling how many dubious looks she and Joseph endured from outsiders. However, because she viewed herself through God's eyes, she was able to see her future from God's perspective. As a result, she knew that generations to come would see the truth and know God had called her to a special role. Any criticism to the contrary was meaningless. It just didn't matter because she found her identity in her Lord, not in her self-esteem or in anyone else's opinion.

Mary's story holds inspiration for anyone who has struggled against criticism. I admire her natural confidence in God that she exhibited at such a young age, and in more far-reaching circumstances than I've faced.

There's another girl in the Bible whose story also makes me go *wow:* Queen Esther. Now, this girl wasn't up against personal attacks to her reputation. Instead, she was forced to step out of the sandals of an exiled Israelite living in Persia and into the shoes of a queen. Talk about intimidating.

Because his former queen had insulted him, King Xerxes was looking for a replacement bride. As it turned out, beautiful Esther was one of the unlucky virgins to be added to Xerxes' harem, where the king took a fancy to her and made her his new queen.

If that weren't awkward enough, Esther soon came to realize her job as queen involved much more than she'd bargained for. Xerxes' top official, egomaniacal Haman, was bent on destroying the Jews, and it was up to Esther to save the day.

I think it's safe to say not too many of us would covet that role. In order to rescue her people, Queen Esther had to approach the king, not once, but several times. Each time meant risking her life because Xerxes didn't have to give her the time of day.

Yet Esther knew she was loved by the King...not the king, but the *King.* And the King would be her confidence in the midst of insecurities.

Like Mary, the young queen felt the normal misgivings any human would: "All the king's officials and even the people in the provinces know that anyone who appears before the king in his inner court without being invited is doomed to die unless the king holds out his gold scepter. And the king has not called for me to come to him for thirty days" (Esther 4:11).

However, when pressed to act in confident assurance that God would equip her for his plans, Esther proved he was able to fit her royal slippers to her feet. She'd have what it would take. She would be enough for her role, because her God was more than enough for her.

Her God-assuredness is evident in her words and actions: "Then Esther sent this reply...: 'Go and gather together all the Jews of Susa and fast for me. Do not eat or drink for three days, night or day. My maids and I will do the same. And then, though it is against the law, I will go in to see the king. If I must die, I must die'" (Esther 4:15-16).

God was her King, not Xerxes. And God provided everything she needed to rise above insecurities and serve an active part in his perfect plan.

These girls knew a thing or two I wish I'd applied sooner, but I hope to help my child learn them early on.

My baby will begin life with tiny socks to fill, but each day we raise him or her we'll be helping this unique person learn to listen to God's voice, to find identity in belonging to Jesus, and to grow confident in his or her own shoes as those shoes grow through the years.

It's a weighty task, sure to be filled with copious joys and tears, and sure to prove us failures unless we look to the One who designed and nurtures us.

*You...kept me from stumbling, so that I would
please you and follow the light that leads to life.*

PSALM 56:13 CEV

CONSIDER THIS...

1. In your early years, who cheered you on? Who did no favors to your self-esteem? Think of one formative memory that instilled doubt in you about your worth. How did that doubt creep into your thoughts as you grew up? How do you counteract it as an adult?

2. Imagine your ideal self, the person you picture being when you're at your full potential, free of the faults and insecurities that trip you up. How is that ideal different from your real self, the person you actually are on a daily basis? What remaining areas of insecurities might you have to address in order to become your ideal self? What role does God play in your self-esteem?

3. Take a look at Psalm 18:32-33. How are the feet of a deer uniquely fitted for the terrain where they live? God made their "shoes" able to walk the ground where he placed them; how does his care for them give you hope that he'll be enough for you as well?

4. Read the first two chapters of Genesis, keeping in mind what it must have been like for Adam and Eve to walk closely with God

as the first two people on earth. They knew no criticism from others, and they lived with the assurance that they were made in God's image. What does it mean to you to be made in the image of God? How should this truth affect your assurance of his acceptance of you?

5. You may be familiar with Hebrews 11:1 (NASB), which gives a wonderful definition of faith: "Faith is the assurance of things hoped for, the conviction of things not seen." Consider it now in the context of your self-esteem. How does the depth of your faith in God affect your confidence about how God views you? How does his view of you, in turn, impact the way you see yourself?

KILL COMPARISON
BEFORE IT KILLS YOU.

I watched in silence as my friend visiting from California adjusted her ponytail for the umpteenth time. It was perfect already, for cryin' out loud. She laid back on her towel and sighed daintily.

My hair couldn't look that silky for anything. I reached up to brush a flyaway—make that frizzy—curl and swallowed another taste of dissatisfaction.

Looking out over the scene at the city pool, my eyes took in the familiar sights of midwestern suburbia. So much less hip than California I was certain, though I'd never been there.

I sighed and looked down at my one-piece swimsuit. Why couldn't I have a bikini too? I would be in junior high that fall. If they wore bikinis at my age on the Pacific beaches, shouldn't I be allowed to usher in such style at the city pool?

I was uneasy enough that summer with a new school and adolescent angst hovering ever-present. Why not kick me while I was down with blatant reminders of everything I already sensed was wrong with me? I'd never fit in in California. Was there any chance left that I could even make it in my own school?

There was no hiding it any longer. No deluding myself that I could pass for cool. Not with unmanageable hair and a wardrobe that was *so* sixth grade. Earlier that afternoon, my CA friend had called my attention to the inadequacies of my clothes when she not-so-subtly asked if my outfit was considered in style around here.

I glanced again at her little nose pointing toward the heavens from where she reclined on her beach towel.

Snob.

I wouldn't want to be her anyway. Not if it meant being a snob.

Yeah, I was much nicer. And nicer was more important, right? I'd never say something tacky to make another person feel bad about herself. Not me. Not super nice me with the bad hair and last year's one-piece.

Life was so unfair.

Who of us hasn't fallen prey to the grass-is-greener mentality?

From our days on the elementary school playground when our efforts at kickball couldn't measure up to Joey's or our bikes didn't have the pretty handlebar streamers like Josie's, we tend to begin the deadly game of comparison at a tender age.

Then again, perhaps you were the Joey or Josie who typically ended up on the winning side of things. Did that stop you from comparing? Probably not.

Even having it all doesn't release most people from the comparison trap, because abundance can develop a dangerous sense of entitlement. And becoming accustomed to having the upper hand can distort a healthy view of ourselves. Just check out the story of the Pharisee and the tax collector in Luke 18:9-14. Outwardly, the Pharisee seemed to have it all. The tax collector, on the other hand, was frowned at wherever he went. But look at who ended up getting the better rap in the Bible.

There's no way to win with comparison. It's a bad deal to get into, but a tough one to avoid. If you always feel like the loser, well...you feel like the loser. And if you always feel like the winner, you easily might wind up belittling others outwardly or within your heart.

Neither outcome fits the character traits God prescribes for us in the Bible.

What tempts us to compare? Why can't we all just get along and be happy?

Something inside me withered that afternoon at the pool. I'd been okay with myself until my misfortunes burned worse than the summer rays. I think as we grow older and experience more of the world, we can't help but lose a little of our innocence. The part of us that's content with simplicity gets chomped on by the green-eyed monster of jealousy and its mentor, the beast of dissatisfaction.

It starts ridiculously early, and for some of us it takes far too long to squelch.

Sad, really. If you notice tiny children much, you probably know how perfectly comfortable they are with themselves. In fact, most toddlers I've met couldn't be prouder of who they are.

But once they realize there's a world of peers out there, the competitive edge kicks in and it's play group nuclear war over Gracie's doll or Avery's sand bucket. You can see the ferociousness on their faces. Why should that kid get something I don't have? Pure and simple toddler logic says he most definitely should *not*.

Comparison comes into play when we think we've gotten a raw deal, and humbling as it may be to admit, we all give in to toddler logic at times. At least I do. I was on the waning side of my twenties before I truly became content with myself and my life as it was.

The prophet Elijah thought he'd gotten a raw deal, and at first glance I don't blame him. His story tells me a thing or two about what to do with my own discontentment.

As God's messenger to the Israelite king Ahab, Elijah worked his tail off speaking truth when truth wasn't welcomed. He sacrificed the comforts of home to live in hiding from evil Ahab and Queen Jezebel, who didn't want to hear his warnings. Meal to meal, he trusted God for his most basic needs.

God was pretty creative in what he provided for Elijah. He gave shelter, sent ravens to bring food to the prophet, and directed Elijah to specific people for help (1 Kings 17).

God also worked miracles through Elijah. By God's power, Elijah stopped and restarted the rain, he made a poor widow's flour and oil last indefinitely, he brought her son back to life, he defeated the queen's favorite idolatrous prophets, and he ran faster than a chariot.

You'd think he'd be flying high on his big wins, but the guy was pooped. In Elijah's vulnerable state, dissatisfaction attacked with a vengeance. The last straw came when Jezebel issued her most terrifying threat:

> Jezebel sent a messenger to Elijah, saying, "May the gods punish me terribly if by this time tomorrow I don't kill you just as you killed those prophets." When Elijah heard this, he was afraid and ran for his life...Then Elijah walked for a whole day into the desert. He sat down under a bush and asked to die. "I have had enough, LORD," he prayed. "Let me die. I am no better than my ancestors." Then he lay down under the tree and slept (1 Kings 19:2-5 NCV).

God saw Elijah's fatigue and asked him what was up: "Elijah! Why are you here?" (1 Kings 19:9 NCV).

Elijah groaned about his lot in life that left him lacking:

> LORD God All-Powerful, I have always served you as well as I could. But the people of Israel have broken their agreement with you, destroyed your altars, and killed your prophets with swords. I am the only prophet left, and now they are trying to kill me, too (1 Kings 19:10 NCV).

No denying it, Elijah had faced his share of struggles. For all the good he'd done, it seemed his enemies still had it better than he did, and it's likely he would have traded places with them. They were the ones with power, money, and influence. Elijah was running for his life, sitting in the desert, and praying to die.

Where's the justice?

Elijah's life was in danger on two fronts. Jezebel wanted him dead, and comparison threatened to destroy his inner life.

God does something interesting then. It's one of my favorite passages in the Bible because it never fails to quiet my comparison complaints. God satisfies Elijah with his own presence, his whisper that quiets the prophet's troubled spirit:

> The LORD said to Elijah, "Go, stand in front of me on the mountain, and I will pass by you." Then a very strong wind blew until it caused the mountains to fall apart and large rocks to break in front of the LORD. But the LORD was not in the wind. After the wind, there was an earthquake, but the LORD was not in the earthquake. After the earthquake, there was a fire, but the LORD was not in the fire. After the fire, there was a quiet, gentle sound. When Elijah heard it, he covered his face with his coat and went out and stood at the entrance to the cave (1 Kings 19:11-13 NCV).

God whispers his previous question again. "Elijah! Why are you here?"

Why would he ask the same thing twice? I think he did that to get Elijah's attention and to focus the man on what was most important. In other words, what was Elijah's purpose? Was he satisfied with God? And would he let God's gentle presence refill him in the unique ways he needed it?

God shows compassion on Elijah and provides someone to take over as prophet, but he also points out that Elijah is not the only one living for God. If Elijah was really going to compare his situation, he ought to know that seven thousand other people in Israel hadn't worshiped Baal either. They were having a tough time too, just like Elijah.

The grass is often greener until you know the truth of someone else's circumstances. Elijah didn't have it as bad as he assumed when he felt so alone. In fact, his miraculous experiences with God were unique and special, even if they came with a hefty set of challenges.

Because of his circumstances, he had blessings in his relationship with God that were perfectly suited to him.

God deals with each of us differently. Our big challenge is to allow him to do what he needs to do in and through us. Nobody has it all, and the grass really isn't greener anywhere than within God's will for each of us. When we let God be God and trust him with the details, there's no comparing what God can do with us.

Elijah really isn't a Bible character to pick on. He lived a stellar life following God. But his story illustrates how much we all need God's deep, quiet presence to satisfy us when we want to gripe.

You might know the parable Jesus told about the servants who compared what their boss paid them. Some worked all day, while others worked only a couple of hours. However, the boss chose to pay them all equally.

> When those hired first came to get their pay, they assumed they would receive more. But they, too, were paid a day's wage. When they received their pay, they protested to the owner, "Those people worked only one hour, and yet you've paid them just as much as you paid us who worked all day in the scorching heat" (Matthew 20:10-12).

Can't you relate? As with Elijah's case, where's the justice?

The boss's response probably wasn't what any of us would choose to hear when we feel slighted. "He answered one of them, 'Friend, I haven't been unfair! Didn't you agree to work all day for the usual wage? Take your money and go. I wanted to pay this last worker the same as you...Should you be jealous because I am kind to others?'" (verses 13-15).

Jesus said, "A person is a fool to store up earthly wealth but not have a rich relationship with God" (Luke 12:21). Our earthly wealth includes many things besides monetary riches. It includes anything that creates discontent that makes us greedy for something God hasn't given to us. Discontent smarts all the more when we see others enjoying what we feel we're missing.

The wealth I desired that summer before seventh grade was for a different image. I felt image poor. I probably could have used a couple of trips to the mall and some extra patience with my hair, but what I needed more was a hug from heaven (or maybe a swat) to set me at ease and remind me what is truly important.

Ultimately, it didn't matter whether my hair was straight or curly, or whether I could qualify as best dressed on the first day of school. But it did matter whether my heart was free of a complaining, greedy attitude.

To sum it up, more of God means less room to be bothered with comparisons. When we trust him, he will provide for all our needs. And he tends to go beyond them and bless us with more as well. He doesn't always give us what we're looking for, but he always gives us what he knows we need.

What is the price of five sparrows—two copper coins? Yet God does not forget a single one of them. And the very hairs on your head are all numbered. So don't be afraid; you are more valuable to God than a whole flock of sparrows.

Luke 12:6-7

CONSIDER THIS...

1. What triggers your tendency to compare yourself to others? In what ways do you feel you fall short? In what ways do you feel you've gotten a better deal than others? How do you cope with dissatisfaction when it hits?

2. It's often easy to spot someone who needs to make him- or herself look better than other people. Do you know anyone like that?

How does that habit affect the way you view that person (your respect level, your trust level, etc.)?

3. Read Matthew 18:1-4, where Jesus talks about the humility of a little child. He does so right after the disciples asked which of them was greatest in the kingdom of heaven. What role does humility play in living free from the temptation to compare yourself with others?

4. Second Corinthians 10:12 speaks powerfully about what standards we're supposed to compare ourselves to. What mistakes do we make when we compare ourselves to human standards versus God's standards? How do God's standards free us from the comparison trap?

5. Romans 8:31-39 are favorite verses for many people because they clearly lay out just how much God loves each of us. How does God's gift of salvation help you rise above the urge to feel dissatisfied with qualities about yourself? What intrinsic value do you have because of God's love for you?

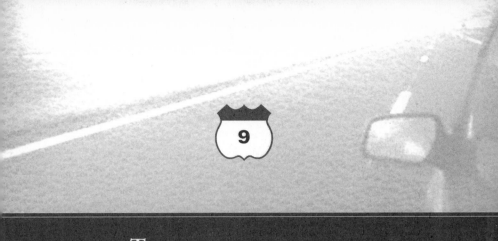

9

I stared into the cave. It stared back.

Dirt like fine gray powder layered the floor, and then only blackness beyond ten feet where the rock walls disappeared into the dark abyss.

We were going in there?

That was half my thinking. The other half said, *Heck, yeah! How fun.*

My high school youth group was on a mission trip at a school in Tennessee, and one afternoon we took a break from our clean-up duties to enjoy a spelunking adventure. I'd never heard of spelunking, but I was about to embark on my first caving trip.

Our guide—let's call him Rocko—said he knew the cave in and out, and since we were stuck trusting him, into the tunnel we ventured, flashlight beams glancing off the walls as a dozen or so of us checked out the underground hideaway's mysteries.

I'm sure Rocko gave a running commentary of the cave as we walked, stumbled, ducked, and scooted our way from one passage to the next, but I don't remember anything except the knowledge that I was utterly vulnerable. The place was huge. On and on we went, sometimes wiggling on our stomachs through tight spaces.

Eventually the tunnel opened to a small chamber, where we gathered and sat for a rest.

Rocko grinned at us. "Okay, lights out."

Had to know that was coming.

One by one each person clicked off the flashlights. The last one made me realize how comforting light is, and it made me look toward Rocko with narrowed eyes. If only we could see each other, he'd for sure catch my threatening look.

We were at his mercy. After leading us to and fro for at least an hour, he'd better prove to be an honest guy. Our booties were buried otherwise. I was too young to die, trapped in this dirt hovel for the rest of time, or at least until another batch of unsuspecting youth groupers tripped over our bones. And prom was coming; I didn't have a date. *Lord,* I prayed, *don't let me die dateless.*

Although common sense told me we'd be fine, a few minutes passed, hidden below the earth, when fear prickled my spine. With light there was little possibility of fumbling our way out on our own. No way without it.

Fortunately, Rocko was on the up and up. He made his point of shocking us, and on we kept going.

Several hours later we emerged, covered in dirt but feeling like Indiana Jones.

Although I still struggle with certain fears, I began to understand a few basics about this emotion that day, namely that fear either traps you or grows you.

Heebie-jeebies, willies, creeps, and jitters. These are a few of a scaredy-cat's least favorite things. I had them all at some point in the cave, even though I loved it. It was an exciting trip, and I'd do it again for sure. With the exception of one harrowing point, my fears were minor and mostly unfounded.

Yet, recalling that day has me considering what a rotten emotion fear is. The bad kind, anyway. There's actually a good kind, but I'll get to that in a minute.

For now, the bad kind.

What triggers your fear reflex? External threats like terrorism, sickness, losing a loved one? Or are your fears more internal, such as fear of rejection, failure, or even success? Whatever your case, you know the feeling. Heartbeat races, palms sweat, chest feels like a ten-ton weight presses on it.

I might have been awakened to the value of pushing through fears in the cave, but I still can shrink under many forms of intimidation, whether or not I manage to hide my anxiety from everyone but myself and God. Fear beckons me to imagine the worst and then hooks me into believing that's the most probable outcome, if not the only one. If I don't squelch it, it ends up convincing me it deserves control. Fear has brainwashing power; I can see how it could drive a person insane.

My little anxieties in the cave were a far cry from true fear that paralyzes and debilitates. Real fear at its worst is a trap with vicious prongs. Three of the most common times it strikes are 1) when we feel our backs are in a corner with no way of escape, like in the cave chamber with the lights out; 2) when we face unknowns, like staring into the mouth of a cave; and 3) when reality isn't so great, and we're afraid it'll only get worse.

We faced a point of genuine danger in the cave when I did imagine the worst. As we neared the end of our journey, we came to a place where the ground ended, and we looked down into an abyss God only knew how deep. A ladder—a very old-looking ladder—stretched ten feet across the gap to where the ground resumed on the other side.

Once across, we stood on a narrow ledge with another rickety ladder leaning vertically against the wall. From there we had to climb straight up, perched over the hole, to another cave room.

A tad unnerving. I wanted to ask Rocko if my father knew he brought me in there.

However, the experience turned into a bonding time for our team.

We'd spent the week in high school antics, but the seriousness of this situation brought out another side of us. To a person, we rose to the occasion and acted like men and women, watching each other's backs and offering a handhold to get everyone safely across and up.

Like I said, fear either traps or grows you.

When fear has us in its clutches, it's easy to be fooled into believing it is in charge. But we have a choice in the matter. God is not a God of fear; he is a God to be feared. The two truths are very different. Different, but related. Fearing God puts all other fears to rest, because when we respect him as the ultimate authority over everything, those other fears diminish in their perceived power. We know nothing happens that he doesn't okay. One type of fear controls the other. It's our decision which to follow as leader.

Speaking of leaders, God chose the Israelite leader Joshua to take over after Moses died. His example is a perfect one for dealing with fear positively. So many stories in the Bible show characters who messed up, but I love that Joshua got it right.

When Joshua stepped into leadership, the nation had spent 40 years wandering in the wilderness. But a new generation had grown up, and it was finally time to take the land God marked as theirs.

Joshua faced all kinds of concerns when he led the Israelites into the Promised Land. He had earned that position through the courage he showed when he scouted the territory and returned full of gusto about moving forward when all but one other man shrank back.

> Two of the men who had explored the land, Joshua son of Nun and Caleb son of Jephunneh...said to all the people of Israel, "The land we traveled through and explored is a wonderful land! And if the LORD is pleased with us, he will bring us safely into that land and give it to us. It is a rich land flowing with milk and honey. Do not rebel against the LORD, and don't be afraid of the people of the land. They are only helpless prey to us! They have no protection, but the LORD is with us! Don't be afraid of them!" (Numbers 14:6-9).

Bountiful as the land was, it was already occupied—with giants, no less. It would take a huge effort to take it over, but Joshua understood that God had set it apart for them. His respect for God as supreme authority translated into courage.

You've got to love an attitude that trades the role of victim for victor. When all others saw the giant inhabitants as oppressors, Joshua and Caleb saw them as prey. These two heroes of faith flipped their defenses into offenses and refused to see themselves as too weak to handle God's plan for them. They faced the same dreads as the other scouts, but no way did they want to miss out on God's fullest life because of a few misgivings. Trust not only translates into courage, but into power as well.

Skip forward to Joshua as leader about to prove God's faithfulness over fear. Poised on the bank of the Jordan River, Joshua had some choices to make. He could either cave to the uncertainties of the future, or he could follow God's direction.

God showed great sensitivity to Joshua's unease. He knew Joshua would face times when he'd feel cornered, clueless as to which way to turn. In this beautiful conversation, we read only God's side, reminding us that God's voice is bigger than Joshua's anxieties. Bigger than ours as well. I like to picture this scene when apprehension hangs on me.

> I will be with you as I was with Moses. I will not fail you or abandon you. Be strong and courageous, for you are the one who will lead these people to possess all the land I swore to their ancestors I would give them. Be strong and very courageous...This is my command—be strong and courageous! Do not be afraid or discouraged. For the LORD your God is with you wherever you go (Joshua 1:5-9).

It's telling that God speaks in the imperative. "Do not be afraid; be strong and courageous." It's a command to do it, not a request to try. God would not command us to do something we cannot do.

Yet this command also reveals compassion for Joshua's emotions.

God knew each problem Joshua would encounter, and his voice gave Joshua the encouragement to move anyway. We see that in the very next verse when Joshua speaks for the first time in this story. He's okay. Able and secure because he met with God before meeting his fears, he issues orders to the leaders under him.

However, his job had only begun. Before long we find him with his back up against a wall, literally and figuratively. Looking across the bank of the Jordan River, he knew they would have to defeat many other people groups before the land would be known as theirs. The city of Jericho was first on the list. They would have to get through the town wall. But in order to get to the wall, they would have to cross the Jordan, and it was at flood stage.

What to do?

With uncertainties piling and unknowns looming, it was more a matter of what God would do—a key element for handling any concern. One by one, God led Joshua and the Israelites through situations that would instigate anyone's trepidation. In each circumstance, God showed himself bigger.

He parted waters, provided people like Rahab to watch their backs, and walked his people through a week-long wall-falling encounter when they could practice their faith despite their fears. It's all told in the first few chapters of Joshua.

Instead of handing the people their land, God required that they face shaky circumstances. Those very circumstances served as catalysts for growing the good fear in God as they witnessed him provide.

Fear of God keeps us more in awe of him than of our bad fears, a huge distinction to remember. Negative fear doesn't have the design of victory to it, as trust in God does. His command to be strong and courageous is a command to keep our healthy fear of him in control of the things that make us shake and quake. With him our backs are never up against a wall. Even though we'll face times when we can't see a solution—like the Israelites on the bank of the overflowing Jordan or me in the darkened cave room—God knows how he'll provide.

If Joshua had caved to his fears, he and the whole nation may have missed experiencing God's saving hand in their lives. Who knows how many more generations would have wandered in the wilderness when they could have been enjoying an amazing new homeland?

Fear of anything besides God makes us wander instead of win. The world is full of reasons to fear, no doubt about it. Life is fragile, and none of us likes to hurt. Seems the more we live, and the more we accept God's gift of adventure, the more opportunities we have to fear. Unknowns breed it, inexplicables breed it, and past hurts breed it. But we only keep heading back to the trap if we wander in our own strength.

There aren't too many greater traps than one's own fears. But fear does not have the design of victory to it, like trust has. God refuses to fail or abandon us. When we fear him above all else, we gain power to stand tall, walk strong, and accept our challenges.

Bad fear means oppression. Fear of God means opportunity, both to grow closer to God and to grow stronger in life. Opportunity doesn't mean ease, and sometimes we get dirty facing our fears. But we must face them anyway.

The only way to escape fear's trap is to grow beyond it.

When it comes to fears, move forward despite the raging in your heart that hollers to go back.

Be an opportunist. Trust God to see you safely to the other side.

How great is the goodness you have stored up for those who fear you. You lavish it on those who come to you for protection, blessing them before the watching world. You hide them in the shelter of your presence, safe from those who conspire against them. You shelter them in your presence, far from accusing tongues.

PSALM 31:19-20

CONSIDER THIS...

1. I asked it before, but I'm asking again—what triggers fear in you? Would you consider yourself a fearful person? Maybe you see it as merely being a worrywart, but worry at its core is really fear that God won't come through for you. How have your fears and worries limited you?

2. I love a good quote. Sometimes hearing one is all I need to shock me out of anxiety mode. Try this one from James Hastings: "Fear is the needle that pierces us that it may carry a thread to bind us to heaven." Relate it to a current fear of yours. How can that fear actually drive you toward God instead of trapping you?

3. Job 28:28 (AMP) says, "The reverential and worshipful fear of the Lord—that is Wisdom." Micah 6:9 (AMP) says, "It is sound wisdom to hear and fear [God's] name." Explain that. How does a person exhibit wisdom by not caving to fear? How is fear of God worshipful? Psalm 27 and Isaiah 33 are great chapters to remind yourself of God's power over enemies. Read them, and focus on his power over whatever real or perceived enemies you face. Let his courage in you be a cause for worship. (Browse the Psalms and Isaiah 41:10,13; 43:1-7 for additional verses on fear.)

4. Fear of God is active, not passive, affecting every aspect of life. Leviticus 19:14,32 and 25:17,36,43 give examples of the fear of God in action. What does it look like on a daily basis? How can you show the fear of God today?

5. John 3:18-21 describes the cause for our deepest fear—being exposed as sinners. Why should people fear this more than anything? Back up now to John 3:16-17. How do these verses calm that greatest fear? Do you have reason to fear being exposed for your sins, or can you put your fear to rest knowing you fear God more and have accepted his gift of salvation through Jesus (the "light" in those verses)?

10

Take it to your knees in prayer.

I was 24 and broke. My second job as a freelance copy editor was earning me enough to cut back to two evenings a week at my third job as a bookstore clerk, but things were still tight. Unexpected bills were piling up, my car was leaking oil faster than I could refill it, and my feet were dragging through the minutes of each exhausting day as I tried to make ends meet. Living was about survival. And my social life? Not even on the radar. Needless to say, I was depressed.

On that positive note, let me add that those breaking years were a few of the most crucial I've faced yet. They taught me to pray and depend on God as never before. And for that reason I wouldn't trade them for anything.

Life had been pretty simple until then. My parents had always done an excellent job providing for my needs, bending over backward to ensure that I had all the financial, emotional, and spiritual support they could offer. But I was suddenly an adult on my own, and lessons clobbered me during those initial postcollege years, sifting my faith and driving me toward new depths in my understanding of God's heart.

Throughout childhood I had been taught to pray for meals, for safety, for provision—for anything that needed attention from above.

However, it wasn't until desperate times hit that I got a real dose of praying for strength through each hour when God continued to answer with silence.

Fortunately, God's silence did not equal his absence.

Are you a praying person? Have you ever been through a season when there were truly no visible answers for an immediate need and God didn't seem to be showing up anytime soon? Sometimes he uses silence to train us to lean on his strength more completely, to trust his character, to change our behavior, to discipline us to want *him* more than his answers, and to show us that he ultimately is the provider for our every need.

Even when we know to pray, it's easy to fall back on prayer as a last resort after the resources we view as more practical have run dry. I was born a worrier, and though I like to think I've made progress in that area, my tendency still is to imagine the worst and stress out from there. Then when I've worked up a good sweat, I remember, *Oh yeah! Might be good to pray about this one.* Duh.

Nineteenth-century pastor and writer A.J. Gordon once said, "You can do more than pray, after you have prayed, but you can never do more than pray until you have prayed." How profound. He must have read his Bible somewhere along the way. Possibly he even came across Philippians 4:6: "Don't worry about anything; instead, pray about everything. Tell God what you need."

Sounds simple enough. Then why is it so hard to put into practice? Well, several factors can complicate our prayer life. A few of those may be sin, lack of faith, or lack of understanding prayer's purpose.

God uses a variety of circumstances to draw us to himself. You may be able to list several ways you've experienced that in your life. In order to understand the role of prayer, we first must understand God's overall goal for us. He wants to save us from our sinful human natures and grow his own character in us. And he wants a loving relationship with us. Communication is a basic requirement in any relationship, and it's no different with God. So he gave us the gift of prayer along with an instruction manual for wielding that amazing weapon.

I had prayed a lot before I learned to pray relentlessly. And I had learned to pray relentlessly before I learned to pray for more intimacy with God instead of merely for faster, greater answers. God wants to show us himself, but often our feeble eyes see him most clearly only after all other powers have been stripped away. By allowing us to face tough things, God uses a method of severe mercy (to borrow from the title of a meaningful book). We want answers; he wants us to have something better: him. And he will let us run ourselves ragged until we release our meager survival techniques into his wise and loving hands. If we'd only pattern ourselves to go to him first, we'd be spared needless heartache and anxiety.

Purposely limiting his own freedom to work, God often waits for us to go to him in prayer because he wants us to take part in his answer. The person who prays much has God's incredible power at his or her disposal. But the person who prays *first* wastes no time or energy in releasing the trigger on God's freedom to respond.

Check out Joshua 10 for proof of how seriously God takes our prayers. Joshua is about to lead his armies into battle, but he's running out of daylight. Verses 12 and 13 tell us, "On the day the LORD gave the Israelites victory over the Amorites, Joshua prayed to the LORD in front of all the people of Israel. He said, 'Let the sun stand still over Gibeon, and the moon over the valley of Aijalon.' So the sun stood still and the moon stayed in place until the nation of Israel had defeated its enemies…The sun stayed in the middle of the sky, and it did not set as on a normal day." God honors our prayers, even to the point of suspending the laws of his universe.

But let's go back to the concept of God's silence. In all of history, no example of this can compare to the hours when his only Son hung on a cross.

In the midst of unspeakable agony, as salty sweat and tears burn the road map of cuts across his body, Jesus cries out to his Father, "My God, my God, why have you abandoned me?" (Matthew 27:46).

Silence.

In my mind's ear it was a silence that screamed.

Did God swoop down in a golden chariot carried along by a mighty bolt of lightning to spare his Son from pain? Nope. Not that day, anyway. But neither did he lose sight of his grand plan to provide us with the only solution to our sin problem. Sin had torn apart our connection to God, and he knew our relationship could be restored only if Jesus paid our price by dying in our place.

While Jesus' body lay in the tomb, how many of his followers—and possibly even his doubters and enemies—thought about his claim that he'd be raised on the third day (see Matthew 16:21 and 20:19)? The passage of time likely challenged them to new or greater faith in him.

Well, when the third morning arrived God answered in a big way. And he proved that he does hear and he definitely cares for our prayers.

Matthew 28:2-3 describes the victory. Imagine the wonder of the scene: "Suddenly there was a great earthquake! For an angel of the Lord came down from heaven, rolled aside the stone, and sat on it. His face shone like lightning, and his clothing was as white as snow."

The angel speaks into the silence of sunrise. "'Don't be afraid!' he said. 'I know you are looking for Jesus, who was crucified. He isn't here! He is risen from the dead, just as he said would happen'" (verses 5-6).

God may hold back an answer because he's working behind the scenes or in our hearts, and he doesn't want us to be cheated out of the joy of waiting closely with him—a joy that's precious despite the pain, and greater than we'd experience from a half-finished answer to our request. Other times he may simply want us to choose to trust him.

Your current challenge may be to pray more, to pray first, or to pray continually. Or it may be to trust more deeply in the One who will respond in his perfect way and time.

God answered Jesus, and he promises to answer us. But first we must enter the battle's front line with prayer.

Never stop praying, especially for others. Always pray by the power of the Spirit. Stay alert and keep praying.

Ephesians 6:18 cev

CONSIDER THIS...

1. Those final two paragraphs challenge you to pray consistently, immediately, and in faith. What do these verses teach about your role in prayer, sin's effects on your communication with God, God's timing, and his promises to you? Psalm 116:1, 146:5-6; Isaiah 30:19; Habakkuk 2:1; Luke 18:1-8; James 5:16-18.

2. Skim Genesis 24, focusing on verses 1-7, 10-27, and 37-52. Did Abraham's servant exhibit enduring prayer or immediate prayer (praying first)? What were the results of his prayer? What need in your life would benefit from your following the servant's example of trusting God's provision?

3. Second Kings 20:1-11 tells of another time God bent the rules of the universe in response to someone's prayer. What happened?

4. Sticking with 2 Kings 20:1-11 for a minute, consider the fact that God also changed his original plans for Hezekiah's life in response to Hezekiah's request. Read Genesis 18:16-33 for another example of God apparently changing his mind. What happened in that situation? Why do you think God was willing to alter his plans after Abraham and Hezekiah prayed?

5. What is one of your most pressing concerns these days? How are

you challenged to pray about it (consider praying with endurance, praying first, or praying more consistently)? Do you truly believe God will show his loving character through his answer? Why or why not? How earnestly are you seeking to know him better through prayer?

11

LIFE'S MESSINESS DIDN'T END WHEN YOU STOPPED MAKING MUD PIES.

Her name was Daniella and she was probably all of four. Black ringlets tumbled around her face, shading dark eyes that gazed up uncertainly. Bird legs and hiking boots peeked out below her dress's ruffled hem. She watched silently as troops of children shivered together, all waiting their turn at the hair-washing station where they would get a few hours' reprieve from the itchy effects of lice. I washed Daniella's hair that chilly day and refused to shiver while she eagerly bent under the bucket of cold water.

Daniella lived in a barrio, a poor village nestled in the hills of Honduras. Home for her was a one-room cardboard shack, which she likely shared with too many family members. Her lovely curls welcomed a new batch of critters later that night when she laid her head on a lumpy mattress.

Daniella likely had experienced more merciless realities in her short lifetime than I'd seen in my quarter century. All those children had. Many weren't truly children anymore; rampant abuse and neglect had stolen any sort of healthy beginning from them.

Though we shared a hemisphere, our childhoods were worlds apart. I spent mine playing on our backyard swing set, running through the sprinkler, and making dandelion-garnished mud pies to line our front steps like an imaginary bakery showcase. Those Honduran kids, many preschool aged, spent their days caring for younger siblings while their mothers worked whatever legal or illegal jobs they could find to earn money for the next day's meal.

If that weren't enough, only one year had passed since Hurricane Mitch devastated the impoverished country. Its wake of terror and loss continued to cripple the Hondurans.

Mitch lashed its fury and proved with sick irony that water doesn't always bring cleanliness. Mudslides flushed through the lower areas, and an aftermath of floods destroyed crops. People clung to loved ones until waves battered loose their grip, sweeping death and destruction throughout the land.

Oh, for the simple purity of a messy mud pie.

Our group of "rich" Americans spent a week offering medical care, prayer, and the hope of salvation. Daniella's isn't the only face branded on my memory from that trip. I see other grubby-faced girls and boys hollering after our bus, celebrating our daily arrival while dodging stray dogs and chickens that littered the dirt road. I see the meek eyes of Fernando's father as he asked for help in raising 12 thousand dollars to cover a liver transplant for his young son—it might as well have been a million to him. I see an ancient-looking fortyish woman crying over the loss of her husband, children, grandchildren, and livelihood. And my memory's eye lingers with disdain on drunken men loitering in doorways, waiting for the next young innocent who didn't belong to them but whom they would take anyway.

They had it all. All the worst effects of a fallible world.

I returned to the States with fresh awareness of just how messy life can get.

I must admit to harboring a sense of entitlement. Perhaps you do as well. In fact, if you're in your twenties, you and your peers have been labeled, fairly or unfairly, the entitlement generation. My sense of entitlement doesn't fill me with pride, but my contriteness hasn't been severe enough to make me relinquish my cozy home and daily comforts for a life of want.

I don't like pain. Not physical, emotional, or spiritual.

I also don't like that none of us escapes pain. No one makes it through life unscarred in some way. Since the world's creation, not one person has lived a pain-free life.

Pain wasn't part of God's desire for the world. The Genesis account of creation describes the Garden of Eden as idyllic, with docile animals and gentle springs of water bubbling up to nourish lush vegetation. No hurricanes or landslides. No abuse or murder. Not even petty theft. It was a haven of peace.

But sin broke Paradise.

Enter imperfect human beings—an oily ingredient that simply doesn't mix with the clear-water purity of a holy God. Ever since Adam and Eve rejected God's standards, we've been at evil's lack of mercy. Sin is a by-product of evil, and pain from any source—whether a natural disaster, a human being, or the devil—is the result.

Yes, evil is alive and kicking. And when it strikes close to home it changes a person forever.

For most of my life I've had a very cerebral idea of evil. It was out there, but it hadn't hit my world to any lasting degree. However, that layer of false security has been stripped away more than once in recent years as I've felt the pain of loved ones dealing with horrific suffering at the hands of wicked people. I don't need to expound on details for your imagination to run through the worst possible scenarios.

You know what? Passing off evil with a solemn acknowledgment of its existence frankly doesn't cut it for me anymore. When loved ones' bodies and emotions are shattered and I can't reverse their terror or remove their hurt, when brokenness contorts their faces and their chests heave in agony, something raw and feral in me threatens to break loose with ballistic fury. I want answers and I want them now. I want a once-and-for-all explanation to reconcile my good God, whom I love with all my screwed-up heart, and this insidious reality of evil.

I'll readily admit that my limited brain doesn't want to accept that sometimes, many times, God does not prevent unspeakable atrocities. TV news broadcasts that fact every day. More than just faraway faces on the screen, those people are real. They have nerve endings that blaze like fire when beaten, emotions that make them retch, and tears that bloat their eyelids.

I want to know *why*…why, why, *WHY* God doesn't sweep down and end such suffering.

You can remind me that these are the effects of sin and we humans brought all of it on ourselves. You can quote Bible verses to me and explain that "the LORD is watching everywhere, keeping his eye on both the evil and the good" (Proverbs 15:3).

There are times when it refuses to make sense to me. Times when even the Bible's explanations feel like mere platitudes. No amount of ranting will change things, but I rant anyway because at those times I simply want God to *fix* things. *Now.*

And then when I'm done, quietness comes. Like the stillness after a storm I'm humbled to realize how often I—"entitled" me—add to the problem. Sin is not some faraway concept. Far too frequently I cause hurt, most often to those I treasure most. I might attempt to rationalize my sins as minor or insignificant in the big scheme of things, but mine alone were enough to send Jesus to the cross.

God understood the extent of our crisis with evil even before he breathed everything into existence. He knew full well that to create a world meant to create evil, because he alone is perfect. Everything else is imperfect, faulty.

So why did he bother? A valid question.

Maybe you've experienced such mind-numbing hurt that you wish he wouldn't have spent the effort to bring you into being. No pile of self-help books can patch up your jagged scars.

God does not take your feelings lightly.

It's hard to understand why God created anything that he knew would wreak havoc in his perfect existence. After all, he had an unmarred, utterly pure realm all to himself. But while that utopia might sound heavenly to us, God wanted to share himself with us. First John 4:8 says, "God is love." He's the real deal. And love, by nature, must extend itself. So he created us to be part of a future so wonderful that it blows away the pain here on earth. Love is not the opposite of evil. Opposite implies equality, and love is wholly greater than evil (1 John 4:4).

This next truth stops me in my ranting tracks: God's plan for us is so complete that he even set the solution to sin in place *before* he created us. And the ransom he gave for us was his own Son, Jesus. He withheld nothing to give us everything:

> Set your hope fully on the grace to be given you when Jesus Christ is revealed...For you know that it was not with perishable things such as silver or gold that you were redeemed from the empty way of life handed down to you from your forefathers, but with the precious blood of Christ...He was chosen before the creation of the world, but was revealed in these last times for your sake (1 Peter 1:13,18-20 NIV).

This may or may not be news to you, but if God destroyed evil today, everyone who hasn't chosen life with him would be lost. So not only would they suffer evil on earth, but they would suffer beyond imagining for eternity. Second Peter 3:9 says, "The Lord is not slow in keeping his promise, as some understand slowness. He is patient with you, not wanting anyone to perish, but everyone to come to repentance" (NIV).

God will destroy evil, but he does nothing halfway. So for now his Son's nail-scarred hand reaches out. He knows what it's like to feel a hole inside.

God calls himself "the LORD who heals you" (Exodus 15:26). Before Jesus died a torturous death in our place, he first spent years healing people and restoring wholeness they had lost, or in some cases had never experienced. His healing is thorough, and the process often draws its own unique pain as he gently cleanses our infected parts and resets our broken insides.

He still withholds nothing to give you everything.

The world gets messier by the day, but evil *is* temporary. If you're God's, this future is yours: "No eye has seen, no ear has heard, and no mind has imagined what God has prepared for those who love him" (1 Corinthians 2:9). And

> In his kindness God called you to share in his eternal glory by means of Christ Jesus. So after you have suffered a little while, he will restore, support and strengthen you, and he will place you on a firm foundation (1 Peter 5:10).

This is the God who fights for you, the One who created an answer to trouble before trouble even began. There is only one Solution to evil. Fortunately, he is the right One.

Look for him in your circumstances. Never stop looking. And when you're at the end of your strength, when you can't even feel anymore...rest. He does not leave us in the dark forever; he has proven that part of his character to his people for thousands of years. That must be what he is doing now.

The end of yourself is a sacred place where God waits. He wants you to see him.

He is there.

The LORD reigns forever, executing judgment from his throne. He will judge the world with justice and rule the nations with fairness. The LORD is a shelter for the oppressed, a refuge in times of trouble. Those who know your name trust in you, for you, O LORD, do not abandon those who search for you.

PSALM 9:7-10

CONSIDER THIS...

1. Although soul-searching can prompt hurtful memories, taking an emotional inventory of your experience with pain can allow God room to work healing in you. And all of us have areas that need his touch. What circumstances and people have caused you pain throughout your life?

2. Do you struggle to make sense of evil? In the past, how have you felt about God's choice not to destroy evil right now? How are your feelings affected knowing that he is giving people more time to turn to him?

3. Brainstorm a list of ways God has shown his love for you throughout your life. You might include names of loved ones, basic provisions of food and clothing, safety, spiritual mentors, or any times when you've sensed his presence. You might want to keep this list and add to it as a reminder that he really is working in the details of your life. Ephesians 1:3-5 states clearly again that God began caring for us before he created us. Read those verses several times until they become personal.

4. Read the following Scriptures regarding the defeat of enemies as well as restoration and healing. What hope do you gain from each? Psalm 76:1-9; 90:13-17; 94:16-23; 120:1-4; 124:1-8; Jeremiah 31:1-14; 1 Corinthians 2:9; Jude 1:5-7. Share your thoughts, good and bad, with God.

5. Read Psalm 18 for a wonderful image of God's fury against those who wish harm on you. Which verses speak most powerfully to you?

12

CONTROL THE CAREER CIRCUS; IT'S STIFLING INSIDE THE TENT.

Ever been to a circus? You know, life under the big top? With a little imagination, you can see activity buzzing in three rings and hear the music and sniff the scents of cotton candy and popcorn.

Got the picture in your head?

Next, check out the players. Decked out in multicolored finery, they are a sight to behold. Trapeze artists and high-wire acts. Lions and ponies and elephants (oh my). And let's not forget the jugglers, the ringmaster, and the clowns. Got to have clowns.

In my version, my breath catches as an acrobat takes a death-defying leap and then catches again when a balloon pops behind me—or was that the lion trainer's whip? I wince when a fire-eater wraps his mouth around a flaming torch and sit mesmerized by the grace of a bareback-pony rider. The whole scene is larger than life, pure adrenaline-pumping excitement, and for a couple of hours I want to be part of it.

But I may be confusing circus life with career life...

Sound weird? Maybe. But maybe not. Not if you love what you do.

Careers come in all forms and functions, but there are a few similarities you can count on from workplace to workplace. You've got your ringmaster who oversees the show and wears a professional face for the outside world. Then there are your daredevil risk-takers who live for the next rush. And how about the animal trainers, along with a few wild beasts who need a whip cracking to keep them in line. Then, of course, we've all met a few clowns at work whose sole purpose seems to be to entertain and get in the way. Finally, there are the onlook-ers. The dreamers who know they have it in them to be great, to awe and astound just like the other performers (I mean, coworkers). But somehow the wanna-bes remain plastered on the bench, not really content but also not willing to accept the challenge to move beyond their comfort zone.

A circus is filled with dreamers and doers, tough training and deep-rooted ambition, complete with its unique set of infighting and politics. Those who get sucked into it live and breathe the lifestyle. There's a great deal of pressure to be the best, to put on a good per-formance, to fool the crowds into thinking there's no fear involved. I imagine life inside the tent can become pretty heated, and when the heat's on, that world can seem pretty stuffy at times.

Sounding more like your office? I'm telling you, the career life can be a circus. You've got to take care not to get dropped without a safety net, or bitten or burned or—worse yet—burned out.

Where do you fit in? A daredevil striving for the top? Perhaps a clown who simply enjoys being part of a team and lightening the mood? Maybe you struggle against the trainer's whip in an effort to prove yourself. Or just possibly you're still dreaming of getting in on the action.

As exciting as the career of your dreams can be, there comes a point when too much time inside the tent becomes confining, limit-ing your scope and fooling you into believing that the career circus is all there is to life.

Although I work from home now, I still feel sucked in by my own career circus. Sure, my "tent" may appear smaller since I no longer sit at a computer linked to a huge network in a big building, and my commute has been reduced from 25 minutes to ten steps. But in many ways, my working world has grown larger over the last few years. Since leaving the office life, I have found my goals expanded. New opportunities have opened up, along with deeper drives to succeed.

Oh, those drives to succeed. So important, yet so deceptive when left unchecked.

Most of my years in an office environment were plenty of fun. I was fortunate to work for great companies with several supervisors I can't say enough good things about. I enjoyed being challenged and energized by others in my field, and let's face it, working alone all day leaves something to be desired in the way of camaraderie. Thank heaven for e-mail!

Even so, I also witnessed my share of corporate politics and groaned more than a few times over issues I didn't agree with but didn't have authority to change. If I had to name my circus role, I think I would have fit best with the jugglers. I learned to balance several tasks at once, but I was never the player flying high for all to see.

Not that a part of me hasn't yearned for life in the spotlight—sometimes *too* big a part of me. Like most people, I have battled plenty of weak moments when I just wanted to feel more important. *I* wanted to be in the center ring, the performer most relied upon to draw crowds, bring in money...soak up attention.

Yep, I can be a sucker for wanting to prove myself. It's part of human nature's drive for success, that quality I mentioned earlier. While ambition is great for pushing us toward our goals, it possesses a destructive nature when allowed to run rampant. A sort of Jekyll and Hyde character.

Think about it: How many people do you know who have never cared about making a name for themselves? I'm talking honestly, wholeheartedly *do not care one iota* about earning any sort of recognition?

If I wore one, my hat would be off to those folks—especially those very few who embrace that attitude while they're still young. Age may tone down the desire to build one's own world, but in most cases not too much.

We all want to be valued. And when you find a career you're passionate about, it can be tough not to focus on it to the detriment of life outside your circus tent. After all, you're young! You've got lots of talent and energy to spare! You've got so much to prove! (There it is again, the idea of wanting to prove something.)

I love what I do. Finding just the right blend of words in a way that's never been expressed, conquering the blank page, making people pause or sit up and listen or laugh or even cry—it's a connection that sends me soaring like an acrobat.

But I've asked myself many times during the past year especially, *Whose world am I trying to build?* If it's my own inside the circus tent of my career, that world will be small indeed. There's only so much breathing room inside a world of our own making, and sooner or later we end up slowly suffocating something vital in us.

It's only when we step outside of ourselves that we're able to see the potential of the bigger world—God's world. His world isn't about our performance. His goal for us isn't to see us make it into the center ring, where we bask in fawning attention over our successes. He won't stand in awe of our guts-and-glory approach to work that prides itself on its own merits.

This book is a step of faith for me in more ways than one. I've been working on the concept for over a year, so naturally I was more than a tad excited to have a chance to finish it and eventually see it on bookstore shelves. Yet here I am, with a mere two months to go before meeting my precious first child, already experiencing labor pains over this book—this other "baby." I care deeply about the health and well-being of both these kids God is blessing me with, yet I'm struggling with questions about my ability to finish this project on time without putting my growing family through the wringer. Am I nuts? Frequently at three a.m., when these thoughts keep me from sleep, I have to wonder.

More and more I'm realizing how much of my identity has been wrapped up in my titles of writer, editor, and now *author.* I've been striving toward that last one since my fourth-grade Young Authors days. But to be honest, this book has me dealing with gut-level questions about whose world I've been working on. Yes, God can speak through my words and touch someone's life. Yes, God might be pleased by my efforts.

But.

But if my goal is in any way to gain recognition for myself rather than pleasing him and focusing on *his* priorities, then this project is a failure in his eyes. That may sound harsh or extreme to some, but not in light of God's overarching purposes.

Through this time of uncertainty about my abilities and the unknowns of the next few months, I can feel God work on my heart in new ways. Each day that ticks closer to "Due Day" has me on my knees with my heart in my throat, learning to release my career goals for the sake of what's greater. Or rather, *who's* greater. God, my husband, our child—all must come before my career ambitions.

Not just in theory, either, but in day-to-day practice. In the end, there will be no center ring accolades if I've settled my priorities on building my own world.

What a relief that God is not focused on building my world, just as he isn't focused on building yours. He isn't constructing a bookshelf in my heavenly mansion to display my publications. My name will not light up celestial storefront windows. There will be no book signings in eternity.

But my heart, my attitudes, my words, and my actions will leave their mark on the people he brings into my life—the souls he wants to love through me. I may see many of those people in heaven. As he's done for you, he has invited me to be part of growing *his* world, which involves prioritizing the goal of showing his love and salvation to others who need it. This little person growing inside me needs a mommy who knows the Lord—whose lord is not herself. The only way that will happen is if I refuse to make my circus tent world the focus of life and choose, instead, to live in the bigger, freeing space of God's world.

Building God's world frees us from the overweening threats of our own ambitions—that part of ourselves that feels the need to prove our worth. God never asks us to prove ourselves. Quite the contrary. He asks us to lose that drive so his Spirit in us has room to reveal himself as our strength.

Ambition has its place for sure. God loves a strong work ethic and can't stand laziness (Proverbs 10:26; 12:11,24; 13:4; 18:9). We can offer God glory in everything we do, including a job well done. But if our ambition for anything besides God takes over our pursuit of God and his priorities, we will end up messed up. And we'll likely drag people we care about down with us. It's a matter of keeping what's most important in its place and refusing to let distractions knock it out of place. Matthew 6:33 records Jesus' guidance: "More than anything else, put God's work first and do what he wants" (CEV).

All these thoughts hit home recently when I was reading through the first chapters in the gospel of Matthew. Two men stood out to me: Jesus and John the Baptist. Jesus, of course, is in a class by himself. But as I studied John's actions, I was struck by his role as well.

As God's appointed man to announce Jesus' coming ministry, John already had his own set of disciples. He could draw the crowds. Jesus himself even said of John, "Of all who have ever lived, none is greater than John the Baptist" (Matthew 11:11). John certainly had human reasons to feel proud of his place. But he showed he was not about building his own world. He was not on a ruthless journey toward the top, and he didn't stomp on people in a quest to be ring-master or to secure the corner office. In fact, he hesitated to baptize Jesus because he knew Jesus held higher authority: "'I am the one who needs to be baptized by you,' he said, 'so why are you coming to me?'" (Matthew 3:14). Those are not the words of someone bloodthirsty for recognition.

Two of John's disciples ended up leaving him to follow Jesus (John 1:35-37). Did he feel deserted or discouraged because someone else was gaining more attention? Not likely, considering that he knew his greater purpose was to point others to Jesus. He probably viewed losing disciples to Jesus' work as a great success.

Now, like John, let's focus more closely on Jesus. After Jesus' baptism, the Holy Spirit led him to the wilderness to be tempted by Satan (Matthew 4:1-11). In his three temptations, Satan targets Jesus' pride as God's Son, an identity that held all the power and prestige anyone could want. Would Jesus try to gain attention to himself by 1) performing the God-sized feat of turning stones into bread, 2) pridefully jumping off the Temple and expecting God to cater to his demands for security, or 3) selling out on God to gain his own wealth and power on earth?

Most of us would have caved to at least one of those seductions. Satan knows human nature well, and he knows just how to "help" us rationalize our mixed motivations that influence our drive for success.

But Jesus stayed true to his Father and kept his eyes on his bigger purpose: to build God's kingdom. Jesus' career, so to speak, while he was on earth involved a brief three-year ministry that required a great deal of hard work. He was no slacker who neglected what he needed to do. But he had his ambition in check, as did John.

Jesus' first action step after his wilderness temptations was to find other team players who were willing to transfer their ambitions to the bigger work he invited them to take part in.

I think there's a lesson in the order of those events. When we're driven to build God's world instead of our own, God can use us in bigger ways. Jesus certainly didn't have to prove himself to God since he *is* God; however, by having his heart's priorities in the right place, he showed he was ready to move ahead in his "career."

God gave you a healthy measure of ambition and drive, so go ahead and pursue your career goals. Just not at the risk of losing the rest of your life over them.

My imagination continues, and I see myself leaving my tent and reentering the bigger world. It's a good one, with horizons extending beyond my scope. A world not confined or controlled by the pressures of trying to soar in my own strength. A world full of potential I have yet to discover. A world I want to offer my child.

And I know at the end of my life, I'll be glad I had the greater courage to make time for a world beyond my career circus of ambition.

[Jesus] said, "Anyone who intends to come with me has to let me lead. You're not in the driver's seat; I am...What good would it do to get everything you want and lose you, the real you? What could you ever trade your soul for?"

MARK 8:34-37 MSG

CONSIDER THIS...

1. Ambition...good or bad? Life is full of trade-offs; what are you giving up to pursue your career goals? How do your career goals line up with or stray from what God might want for you? What temptations in your career have the power to take your focus off God's highest goals for you? What could your goals cost you or others?

2. In what ways have you caught yourself trying to prove something to yourself or others? Did you realize it at the time? Did anyone else? Author Ken Davis wrote a book called *Fire Up Your Life!: Living with Nothing to Prove, Nothing to Hide, and Nothing to Lose.* How does living to build God's world instead of your own free you to live with nothing to prove, hide, or lose? How can it free you from unhealthy competition with difficult supervisors and coworkers?

3. John the Baptist summed up his top priority with these words about Jesus: "He must become greater and greater, and I must

become less and less" (John 3:30). The Message words this verse in a way that paints a picture of the circus tent of your career: "This is the assigned moment for him to move into the center, while I slip off to the sidelines." Explain what less of yourself and more of God might look like in your daily work life. Does that concept intrigue you, excite you, or frighten you? Why?

4. God wants to use your training—whether it's a high school diploma, college degree, or life experience—to build his world. Read Matthew 4:18-22, which shows Jesus recruiting several of his disciples. How might their knowledge and experience as fishermen have prepared them in unique ways to be his right-hand men? (Consider the challenges and the lifestyle of a fisherman back then.) How can God use your background in his work?

5. Aiming high for raises and promotions might seem responsible, and there's value in taking your job seriously, as well as your responsibility to earn a living. But explain how it reveals a level of irresponsibility to let your career goals usurp priorities God values more. What worth do you place on intangible earnings such as quality of life, integrity, solid relationships, and rest and relaxation time? Consider King Solomon's words in Ecclesiastes 2:9-11,18-26; 11:9. What are you working for that will last beyond your lifetime? How about into eternity?

13

Everyone has issues; own yours.

I'm not a fan of housework. Imagining the brushes and mops and vacuums and dust rags and sponges and bottles of chemicals filling our closets and cabinets makes my heart sink a little.

Don't get me wrong; I'm not afraid of hard work, and I can put in a good day's effort as well as anyone. A solid work ethic is super important, and our motto around our house is "Work hard, play hard." From manual labor to brain labor, I'm your gal for any number of jobs.

But when I dust one day only to look at a new layer of film covering the furniture the next, it gets old, you know? Have you ever stopped to count the surfaces in your home? *Endless* places for dust to collect. And the bathrooms. Oh, the bathrooms. My mother was a crafty woman to hand off that duty to my siblings and me when we were old enough to do a decent job. Can't say I blame her. Bathrooms are dirty, dirty work. I guarantee my own kids will inherit that task as soon as I can get them birthed and trained.

Steve's no curmudgeon when it comes to his part of the housework, and he even entertains my idea to hire a cleaner—just as soon as I start rolling in the dough. (So thanks for buying this book. One step closer to reaching my goal before I'm dead.) But for now, it's up to our four hands to maintain our home.

Welcome to real life, Erin.

If I had to pick a favorite cleaning chore, it would be laundry for sure. The weekends are typically wash days around here. That's when Steve and I tag team with each other and the washer and dryer to clean up our act for the week ahead.

Maybe it's the put-it-away-and-forget-it-till-it's-done aspect that I like. Plus, everything comes out so fresh and warm and cozy. There's nothing like stuffing in sweat-dried, week-old workout clothes and other grungy items, only to take them out smelling mountain fresh or ocean breezy. And the folding and putting away part is like prepping ourselves with clean armor for heading into the demands of the work week the next morning.

You may be wondering what metaphor for life could possibly tie into all this. Who really cares about my laundry detail? Well, here it is:

If only it were as easy to clean up, fold up, and put up our other kinds of dirty laundry—those emotional articles that lurk stinking and worn at the bottom of the soul.

Issues. Hang-ups. Skeletons in the closet. Baggage. Call it what you like; it's all the same. Emotional dirty laundry by any name stinks.

And we've all got it. None of us is alone in our screwed-up state. An odd sort of comfort, don't you think? However, when one of our issues airs its stench for all to smell, our faces flare with humiliation as red as the emotional scars we attempt to hide.

What do I mean by *issues?* Well, they go beyond temperament quirks like chattiness or shyness, stubbornness or timidity. Those idio-syncrasies add charm and character to our personalities and endear us to others, despite the trying nature they occasionally entail.

A true issue is something that gets in the way of our relationships, our ability to function in healthy interpersonal ways, and our outlook

on life. They go deeper than mere personality traits and can even inter-
fere with someone's authentic personality. They might include things
like an obsessive need for control, an overpowering fear, an unhealed
addiction or compulsion, or an unrestrained anger problem.

Surely you've met someone whose critical nature hinders their job
performance, or someone whose perfectionist bent keeps other people
at arm's length for fear of never measuring up. Quite possibly you've
run across a control freak or two, and probably a rage-aholic as well.
How about someone who can't stand up for herself or someone who
thinks the world is out to get him?

They're serious business, those issues.

They trip us up and paralyze our emotions. They keep us from
enjoying the fullest life God intended for us, and they can hinder us
from reaching our greatest potential to impact other lives. Our issues
come in endless forms and labels, from just as many sources, and we
all find coping mechanisms to deal with them.

And there's one thing they have in common: They're all rooted in
past hurts.

No matter if you've come out of a Beaver Cleaver childhood or
something more along the lines of *Married with Children* (or worse),
you did not escape unscathed in some way. Because there's no perfect
parent, there's no perfect upbringing. Whiffing at least a wee bit of
dysfunction on our trek through the laundry room of life is part of
our deal as human beings.

A past stained by abuse or neglect could leave a person unable to
trust. An inability to please a difficult parent could show up later in
low self-esteem or a defensive spirit, while too much coddling from
indulgent parents could develop a me-first attitude that gets in the way
of career and personal life. Most of us probably recall ridicule from
peers, negative feedback from teachers, or any number of random
experiences that managed to leave their marks deep on our psyches.

And then there's the baggage that comes from our own mistakes.
Behaviors and words and attitudes we're not proud of. The ones that
hurt others, and the ones we're still paying for and cringing over.

The ones we'd give anything to redo, or at least wipe from anyone's memory.

Ugh.

It's all dirty laundry. And it stinks when it continues to sour inside us, eventually creating distance between us and those around us who slowly back away for need of fresher space. One thing's for sure: Letting our dirt collect too long inevitably catches up with us. It clutters our path in life and relationships, blocking out freshness we could otherwise enjoy.

We may try to stuff away those hurts like laundry in a hamper or brush them aside like annoying dust, but there are very few ways to contain a mess for long, emotional ones included. And like the dust I hate, a bad stench permeates tiny crevices and reveals itself in endless ways.

We all face times when we're overdue for old-fashioned spring cleaning. It requires hard work, commitment, and time, but investing in our own emotional maintenance can save a lot of wasted energy and heartache down the road.

So, what to do…

Fortunately, there's a place we can turn to for assistance with our self-cleaning regimen. Before we get into that, however, let's clarify a few things about emotional issues. First off, we know we all have them. Part of life. Unavoidable as imperfect humans.

We've covered that part; it's a given.

However, before any clean-up can be done, a person has to know what his or her hang-ups are. We've each got to be willing to deal honestly with ourselves and admit where our messes have collected inside us—a tough task to do because our natural instinct, especially when covering over hurts, is to go into self-protection mode.

Let's face it, life can be painful. To top it off, the clean-up process can be just as painful when we've got to relive heartaches in order to move beyond them. Who wants to compound pain with pain?

But whether our issues stem from our own mistakes or from someone else's, there comes a point, now that we're adults, when we have to take responsibility regardless of whatever hurts us. We have to own our issues before we can fully deal with them. We may not like 'em, but they're ours.

Approaching our weak areas honestly despite our pull to defend them takes conscious effort and sometimes more strength than we have on our own.

Which brings us back to the place we can turn for the ultimate emotional clean-up.

Back in the prophet Ezekiel's day, God's people, the Israelites, needed some heavenly housework done (emotionally speaking). They'd been scattered and exiled, and their lives were in shambles. Their relationship with God was not what it needed to be, and as a result they suffered big time from their enemies as well as from their own failures.

But God declared his role as their master Cleaner:

> Here's what I'm going to do: I'm going to…pour pure water over you and scrub you clean. I'll give you a new heart, put a new spirit in you. I'll remove the stone heart from your body and replace it with a heart that's God-willed, not self-willed. I'll put my Spirit in you and make it possible for you to do what I tell you and live by my commands…You'll be my people! I'll be your God! (Ezekiel 36:24-28 MSG).

Do you see what God did there? He covered several bases in these few words. For starters, he showed the extent of the cleaning process. It often requires some scrubbing, more than just a once-over-lightly. Scrubbing takes extra effort, and it can leave us feeling raw for a bit, but in the long run we're healthier for it.

Next he dealt with their stony hearts that kept them living in self-protection instead of self-honesty. Stone is rough and impenetrable. Great for building walls, but not for an impressionable human heart. Any issue we have eventually reaches our heart, where it impacts our very life's blood, our ability to process life in healthy ways. By reforming our injured hearts, he recreates our ability to handle life productively.

And finally, God let the Israelites know it's impossible to live his way without receiving his cleaning. We knock the dirty laundry pile down to manageable size by staying on track with him. We need his Spirit within us if we're ever going to break free from the perpetual spin cycle of old and moldy patterns. Only he can rinse us clean.

But we really have to want it.

Fast-forward to the New Testament book of John. Chapter 5:1-15 tells one of my favorite stories of God's cleansing power, and what exactly our part is in it.

It begins when Jesus approaches a lame man near a pool. This man had been sick for 38 years, long enough to be worn out over a burden he couldn't shed on his own. Jesus wasn't surprised to find this man; in fact, their encounter was a preplanned God moment. Jesus knew the man had been ill for a long time, and he would be either highly motivated to do his part to turn his life around or resigned to cling to his issues for the remainder of his days.

Which would it be?

Jesus offers the man the same test he offers you and me: "Would you like to get well?" (verse 6).

Such a simple question, yet one that held profound power. How much did it mean to the man to experience true freedom?

Such a simple question, yet one that insisted on an action reaction from the sick man.

Well, the guy didn't catch on right away. "'I can't, sir,' the sick man said, 'for I have no one to put me into the pool when the water bubbles up. Someone else always gets there ahead of me'" (verse 7).

A classic case of resignation. He knew he needed help, but no help had come along for so many years. Decades spent on the sidelines, alone in his grief, had left him feeling separated from everyone else. Cast aside and uncared for, he surely battled feelings of unworthiness as he lay there hour after hour watching others carry on with life as usual, laughing and thriving and not stopping to notice his suffering.

Worse than his physical brokenness, his heart and spirit had been trampled. And because he'd felt dirty and hurt for so long, he figured he'd feel dirty and hurt forever.

As we would expect, Jesus had the perfect response for the man, just as he has for us: "Stand up, pick up your mat, and walk!" (verse 8).

With that command, Jesus empowered the man into realizing he had a part in cleaning up his own troubles. The command wasn't an "If you think you can do it" request.

Hardly.

Jesus' command took for granted that the man had a choice to make, one that he was fully capable of making. But notice also that Jesus didn't leave the poor guy powerless. Jesus' close presence provided the strength the man had needed all along.

In a true lightbulb moment, the man got it: "Instantly, [he] was healed! He rolled up his sleeping mat and began walking!" (verse 9).

Okay, so you may be thinking that our clean-up process doesn't usually happen quite so fast. At least not from our viewpoint, nor from our therapy bills. But from Jesus' viewpoint the man's healing was a done deal.

As is ours from God's perspective.

Oswald Chambers commented on this very phenomenon—God's instant help as soon as we move toward him—in his classic devotional *My Utmost for His Highest:*

> We all have any number of visions and ideals when we are young, but sooner or later we find that we have no power to make them real. We cannot do the things we long to do, and we are apt to settle down to the visions and ideals as dead, and God has to come and say—"Arise from the dead." When the inspiration of God does come, it comes with such miraculous power that we are able to arise from the dead and do the impossible thing. The remarkable thing about spiritual initiative is that the life comes after we do the "bucking up." God does not give us overcoming life; He gives us life *as we overcome*...If we will do the

overcoming, we shall find we are inspired of God because He gives life immediately."[1]

Just because our healing takes time doesn't negate the sureness of God's ability to make it happen. His course of healing might not be the method we expect, but it is always the best course.

And he wants those who belong to him to claim him as theirs. If you're his, then he is yours as well, along with every resource he has for helping you work through whatever life has dealt you.

But you've got to welcome him close and stick with him for the process. No halfhearted once-over-lightlies when he's at work. That's tough to do, but there's a precious intimacy that grows between God and one of his children he's working to refine, an intimacy that can't be developed any other way.

You know what makes this story of Jesus healing the lame man even sweeter? It happened on the Sabbath, God's set-aside day of rest. Can you imagine how rested the man's soul must have felt that day? Sure, he'd been reclining for years, but he'd only grown more exhausted from the burden on his heart. No doubt that Sabbath day ushered in a deep-down, soul-replenishing rest he'd never experienced.

Imagine that kind of rest in your life.

We can be assured that God more than makes up for the areas we lack. His resources are ours when we belong to him. When we trust his ways and commit ourselves to his clean-up process, we'll enjoy a life that sparkles like we never thought possible.

What about you and that issue that won't go away? How long will you wait, settling for less than all God wants for you? Procrastinating can carry tragic costs. Don't risk looking back on these years, wishing you'd addressed your issue sooner.

No one but you can commit to work through it.

Admit it. Own it. Together with God, do the work to clean it.

Then move on from it into satisfying rest.

*I scrub my hands with purest soap, then join hands with
the others in the great circle, dancing around your altar,
GOD, singing God-songs at the top of my lungs, telling
God-stories. GOD, I love living with you; your house
glows with your glory. When it's time for spring cleaning,
don't sweep me out...You know I've been aboveboard
with you; now be aboveboard with me. I'm on the
level with you, GOD; I bless you every chance I get.*

PSALM 26:6-12 MSG

CONSIDER THIS...

1. Think back through your growing up years. Who let you down? How were you let down? Maybe your heart still yearns to know you are loveable, able to please. Maybe that longing shows itself in workaholism, perfectionism, criticism, or some other ism. What specifically would you like God to do to heal your emotions? Now turn the tables: Who have you let down? How do those mistakes still affect you?

2. It's easy for most of us to pick up on other people's hang-ups. Not so easy to see, much less admit to, our own. How honest are you about your emotional areas that could use some growing and healing? What positive and negative feedback about yourself have you received from those who know you? Do you view those comments as opportunities for growth or reasons to feel humbled or embarrassed?

3. Okay, now for the issues that are direct results of our own decisions. What does 1 John 1:5-10 say about the importance of being honest with God and with ourselves when it comes to dealing with our past mistakes? Let's face it, we've all done things we're not proud of, things that still haunt us. What verses or phrases in Psalm 51 offer you hope that God can clean up the messy areas inside you?

4. According to Luke 6:46-49, what role does our obedience to God's ways affect our ability to make a difference for him in the world? How about 2 Timothy 2:21?

5. In the midst of dealing with our "laundry," we need reminders that God isn't finished with his work in us. What encouragements do these Scriptures offer that help you know God is still working in you? Psalm 27; 103; 147:1-11; Philippians 1:6. Check out Luke 6:6-10; 7:1-17 for more stories of God's healing power over people's struggles. In what ways do you identify with those people?

14

Play it positive.

I have an attitude problem. Life doesn't feel fair at the moment, even though I know my gripes are somewhat petty in the big scheme of things.

It's the wee hours of the morning, and I haven't slept since 10:30 last night. However, the rest of the household, guests and all, slumber peacefully. Even my new baby boy is finally snoring quietly. For now. (Yes, Paxton made his grand entrance two and a half weeks ago.)

I fear for the next person who tells me how much I need sleep.

I love my baby. I love his sweet milk breath and his soft cheek against mine during his late-night feedings, but I could use some space between us right now. After a couple of weeks of choppy sleep—following the last two months of pregnancy with little comfortable rest—this feels more like bondage than bonding. Other responsibilities press on me as well, and I want to shout for somebody to take my precious Paxton long enough so I can close my eyes for more than five minutes at a stretch.

My work as a mother has only begun, but I'm already feeling its never-ending quality. Guilt mixes with joy as I battle my current negativity. A brand-new, healthy boy! Cause for incredible joy. But along with this tiny blessing comes a price tag that's going to cost me time, energy, and discipline like I've never had to expend.

Guilt sets in when I wonder how I can complain at all during this miraculous season. I could have real problems. My troubles merely revolve around finding time to meet work deadlines while adjusting to a miniature, squalling stranger.

Before Pax was born, when the crunch of deadlines began to loom, I realized that my attitude would serve as an asset or a liability during this balancing phase. I reminded myself that God is in the timing of everything, and it's in his strength that anything will get done. I told myself to remember how much I love to write and how much I've been looking forward to having this baby.

Yet right now my attitude isn't so bright. Not only that, but there's a vicious part of me that actually *wants* to snap, to allow myself the brief release of negative energy even if it isn't the best reaction. I know this desire is wrong, but I only partly care.

Well, that part of me is speaking louder now, and I'm thinking it's time to kick my attitude back into shape. I can either help or hinder my success by simply readjusting my outlook. Those readjustments seem endless, but I know it's time—yet one more time—to call my attitude to account.

Attitude, shmattitude. Okay, so I'm not over it yet.

I've always been prone to bad attitudes. Sure, I can be sweet and compliant, easy to please, nondemanding...

When things are going according to plan. My plan.

But when life gets off kilter and I feel my control begin to slip, I'm not always the picture of tranquility.

As a young child, I tended to be a pleaser. Being liked by everyone was of utmost importance, and I viewed agreeability as one of the highest character traits, to my own detriment. Of course, I didn't think in those words, but they sum up my basic approach to dealing with people.

However, I do remember one of the first times I'd had enough and let someone know it. I was in junior high, which probably accounted for my sudden boldness. A friend and I were doing homework at the public library (always the bookworm), and for some reason not worth remembering, the librarian had gotten on my last nerve.

With all the fierceness I could muster, I barked an impatient comment to her. She reacted the way I wanted, and I got one of my first tastes of the power of *attitude*.

What a thrill! Twisted, perhaps, but a thrill nonetheless to realize that formerly timid me could create waves with a snarling upper lip and a dose of sarcasm.

Although my friend's expression registered the shock I felt, I was secretly proud.

Until shame set in. I hadn't been raised to talk to adults in that tone. What would my parents think? Such a bad one, I was.

Although it's a fairly innocent story, that experience showed me clearly the impact of attitude for better or worse. I can't say the shame I felt that day cleansed me of all attitude problems since. Quite the opposite, actually. Overall I'm a nice person, but I can bare my teeth more often than I think a Christian needs to, and my bark can be savage if I let it have its full voice.

However, the resulting shame still reminds me I'd better watch myself, because an unchecked attitude is poison to the spirit as well as to relationships with God and others. I cringe now remembering times I acted with unnecessary defensiveness or snarkiness, and I pray that God's mercy will blot those same memories from the minds of people who witnessed them. Those juvenile exhibitions belong back in junior high; they aren't tolerated by others as we enter our twenties.

The word *attitude* conjures a couple of different ideas. First of all, attitude involves a positive or negative outlook, the old saying about seeing the glass half full or half empty. The word's other connotation lines up with my fit-to-be-tied snappishness, the type that earns comments like, "Dude, that chick's got attitude."

Much like the issue of perspective we dealt with in the first chapter, our attitudes have a snowball effect to the good or bad.

Here's what I mean. Given the same set of circumstances, if I remain calm and think positively, I'm much more able to handle glitches that crop up. On the other hand, when I let myself get embroiled in the day's stresses, I end up weakened and encumbered, unable to maintain a proactive perspective. When I give that up, I'm headed downhill fast, losing even more of my withered energy reserves. Luxuries I can't afford to waste.

Unfortunately, our human natures don't always listen to reason or follow the wisest course of action. Sometimes—say, after the umpteenth night of sleep deprivation—we don't give a hoot about making the best decision because a foul mood has already moved in and planted roots.

That's where I am today, although the adult side of me knows I can't get away with it for long. No one deserves to enjoy me in my current state, so something's got to change whether I have energy or not.

Fortunately, the longer I know God, the more I'm learning to go to him with every concern. So with a desperate prayer, back to the Bible I go.

God cares a great deal about our attitudes. In fact, he understands the temptation to cop one as a coping mechanism. Let's face it, there's something satisfying about spouting off or giving in to a pity party. But the temporary thrill of making others yield to us has a dark side, which comes in the form of shame. Our sin natures work that way; what we think will feel good oftentimes provides only a short-term rush that fades into well-deserved guilt.

The apostle Paul acknowledged this duality in Romans 7:14-24 (MSG):

> Yes. I'm full of myself—after all, I've spent a long time in
> sin's prison. What I don't understand about myself is that
> I decide one way, but then I act another, doing things I
> absolutely despise...If the power of sin within me keeps

sabotaging my best intentions, I obviously need help! I realize that I don't have what it takes. I can will it, but I can't do
it. I decide to do good, but I don't really do it; I decide not to
do bad, but then I do it anyway. My decisions, such as they
are, don't result in actions. Something has gone wrong deep
within me and gets the better of me every time. It happens
so regularly that it's predictable. The moment I decide to
do good, sin is there to trip me up. I truly delight in God's
commands, but it's pretty obvious that not all of me joins
in that delight. Parts of me covertly rebel, and just when I
least expect it, they take charge. I've tried everything and
nothing helps. I'm at the end of my rope.

These verses tell me that my attitude problems are linked to pride.
What gall I have to dump my sin nature in someone else's lap. What
nerve to subject others to my moments of spoiled character. The guilt
I feel is God's answering Spirit within me, pointing out that I've been
full of myself again.

When our words and actions don't reflect God's character, they're
bound to hurt someone, whether those people are God, others, or
ourselves. We are not given the freedom to cause that kind of pain,
no matter how ballistic we feel.

Wrong attitudes are exhausting. Like all sin, they wear out the
sinner as much, if not more, than the ones who dare to cross paths with
that person. I know this firsthand right now, because I need a break
from myself more than from my tiring circumstances. I do myself no
favors if I continue on my negative path.

So what's the solution? Try as I might to overcome my failings, I'm
stuck with them unless I go to the Source of real help.

As desperate for relief from himself as I am, Paul discovered that
Source, and he tips us off to it: "Is there no one who can do anything
for me? Isn't that the real question? The answer, thank God, is that
Jesus Christ can and does. He acted to set things right in this life of
contradictions where I want to serve God with all my heart and mind,

but am pulled by the influence of sin to do something totally different" (Romans 7:24-25 MSG).

Once again, Jesus is the answer.

Yes, I need sleep. Yes, I have a lot on my plate. But taking my junk to Jesus is always the first best thing I can do. His Spirit in me is a powerful energy extender and a calming balm to my frazzled emotions. I've felt this in the past, and I know deep down that my first order of business must be with him. He understands my weariness and my humanness because he lived within the limits of a human body. He knows what it's like to be twentysomething, and he knows just what we need for refreshment.

He is our attitude adjuster.

To counteract our humanness intruding on our attitudes, we need to "throw off [our] old sinful nature and [our] former way of life, which is corrupted…Instead, let the Spirit renew [our] thoughts and attitudes" (Ephesians 4:22-23).

It might sound simplistic, but isn't simplicity what we need when we feel out of control? Just like God to know that.

By asking God to transform our attitudes, we choose to operate in his strength, which defies our human strength. In releasing a bad mood to him, we invite a positive atmosphere around us, which carries us safely above the snowball careening downhill.

Wow. To think I could actually be a joy today instead of a drain. Quite a concept. There's still work to do, and I'm still tired. But it's time to grow up. Someone has to be the adult, and Pax isn't volunteering. If I'm going to learn this parenting thing, I'd better follow the lead of my heavenly Parent who knows all.

He's got my day covered, just as he has yours in hand. That truth in itself is enough for a lifetime of positive thinking. Somehow he will be enough for me, and somehow he'll help me keep from succumbing to negativity. After all, I have so much to be positive about. I'll have my moments, of course. Probably sooner than I'd like. Probably sooner than my family would appreciate! But each day reinforces to me the value of arming myself with positive attitudes. It's as difficult and as simple as that.

May your attitude today be marked by gratitude for the simplicity of Jesus' strength in you.

Oh…(yawn)…and may you sleep.

— — — — — — —

The word of God is living and active. Sharper than any double-edged sword, it penetrates even to dividing soul and spirit, joints and marrow; it judges the thoughts and attitudes of the heart.

HEBREWS 4:12 NIV

CONSIDER THIS…

1. How often do you catch yourself feeling guilty about something you said or did out of a bad attitude? Think of a time when your attitude hurt someone else, God, or yourself. Do you identify with the dual emotions of temporary satisfaction mixed with guilt? How often do you stop a bad attitude before it snowballs out of control?

2. What types of circumstances and people trigger an attitude problem in you? Consider your pet peeves; these are great starting points for bad attitudes. Would you consider yourself a glass half full or half empty person? Besides shame and guilt, what are some additional repercussions of negativity?

3. "The sinful nature desires what is contrary to the Spirit, and the Spirit what is contrary to the sinful nature. They are in conflict with each other, so that you do not do what you want" (Galatians 5:17 NIV). This verse is similar to Romans 7:14-24. Can you recognize the Holy Spirit's reminders to you to live by his character

instead of by your own? How is your day affected when you're running on your own resources instead of on his?

4.   Read Philippians 2:1-11. What characteristics did Jesus show through his attitude? How did God take care of Jesus (see verses 9-11)? What hope does that offer that he'll be faithful to care for you when you keep your attitude in line with his character? Have you ever considered pride as a root of attitude troubles? How does an others-focused life nip attitude problems in the bud?

5.   Consider Romans 14:17-18: "The Kingdom of God is…a matter of…living a life of goodness and peace and joy in the Holy Spirit. If you serve Christ with this attitude, you will please God, and others will approve of you, too." Also take a look at Romans 15:1-7. What benefits do we enjoy (for example, peace) when we make God our priority and strive to put others' needs above our own?

15

MOVE BEYOND THE PIT OF REGRET.

Few things are as draining as a big old regret.

Not the piddly variety that includes scarfing down those last two pieces of cake or pocketing the twenty you found in the neighbor's yard or borrowing your roommate's MP3 player without asking.

No, I'm referring to the big ones that haunt you in the middle of the night. The mistakes you long to hide from others and the ones that cost you relationships with others. The ones that set you on a different path than what you spent your childhood dreaming about. The ones you'd give anything to take back.

The *regrets*.

Oh, what we'd all give for a life free of them.

They'll suck the steam right out of us with little mercy and no apology, casting us to the bottom of a dried-up well of dashed dreams and even shattered hearts. They can bury us in guilt and cost us more than we expected, leaving us to feel like failures simply because of a bad decision.

Then again, sometimes they flood us when we fail to make a decision at all. I like to call those regrets the shoulda-woulda-couldas because they embody the hopes we'll never see to fruition because we didn't take the necessary risks to make them happen.

Messed opportunities and missed opportunities. Two kinds of regrets that remind us that every choice matters and that we have only one brief life on earth to make the most of.

Yet reality lets us know every day how imperfect we are, and we know it's a pipe dream to think we can live free of all regret. Does that mean we're stuck in the desert with our mistakes, bound forever to memories of ourselves that make us gasp for relief?

Well, anyone who takes God at his word will know that he offers an oasis of freedom beyond even our biggest regrets.

I'm referring to a little verb with amazing power. It's a word used often in Christianese circles, a word thirsted for by sinners the world over.

It's the word *redeem,* and God is all about it.

Peter.

Remember him? One of Jesus' closest disciples, Peter was something of a loose cannon in his younger days. His heart was golden and full of passion, but if ever there was a child to swing from the rafters in Sunday school (although he was Jewish), or a youngster to usher in his generation to the throes of ADHD, Peter was the boy for the job.

He had quite a list of things to make you go *Ew. Yikes. Yowza.* He was a master of impulse decisions that would make most people shudder over the same mistakes. However, his story should give any of us hope that God can move us beyond the past.

Also known as Simon, Peter was one to act first, maybe think later. From attempting to correct Jesus (Mark 8:31-33) to chopping off a man's ear in Jesus' defense (John 18:1-11), Peter was a reprimand waiting to happen. He was a simple fisherman who wanted to do big things, and although his heart was mostly on the right track, his common sense often lagged behind. Quick to jump up and follow Jesus, he was just as quick to jump out of the boat and walk on water in faith (Matthew 14:28-31). But his faith needed to grow before he could be truly faithful as a follower of Christ. In the learning time, he made many judgment errors.

No doubt his biggest cause for regret came the night before Jesus was crucified. It was the evening of the Last Supper, and Peter joined Jesus and the other disciples for their last time together before Jesus' death.

A subdued atmosphere hovered in the room as each man tuned his ears to their Lord's parting words. Years spent in close community had narrowed the gaps between them, and their mutual care for one another deepened the mood and heightened their sensitivity to every word. It was a night overflowing with meaning, and no doubt the weight of the world on Jesus' heart cast a shadow on them all, even if they still didn't fully comprehend the import of the coming weekend.

And then Jesus' shocking words: "I will be with you only a little longer" (John 13:33).

Brows furrowed with questions. Hearts pounded with anxiety. Their time together had been life changing; this foreshadowing of loss surely was not welcome.

As usual the first to speak, Peter asked Jesus where he was going, to which Jesus replied, "'You can't go with me now, but you will follow me later.'

"'But why can't I come now, Lord?' [Peter] asked. 'I'm ready to die for you.'"

Then Jesus had to set him straight. "Die for me? I tell you the truth, Peter—before the rooster crows tomorrow morning, you will deny three times that you even know me" (John 13:36-38).

It's bad enough to be smacked with regret after the fact, but to feel it before the sin was even committed must have sent shock waves of shame through Peter. Jesus' words to Peter would be like him telling you that you will cheat on your spouse, or you will abuse a loved one, or you will destroy someone's life. How would you come to grips with such a bleak prediction of your future? Most likely you'd scramble for footholds to climb out of the well of regret.

Peter's response was instantaneous. "'No!' [he] declared emphatically. 'Even if I have to die with you, I will never deny you!'" (Mark 14:31).

Words count for only so much, though.

After the Last Supper, Peter went with Jesus to the Garden of Gethsemane, where Jesus warned him and the other disciples to pray against giving in to temptation (Luke 22:40). Jesus knew their faithfulness would soon be tested severely.

The night went downhill from there.

> [Jesus] took Peter, James, and John with him, and he became deeply troubled and distressed. He told them, "My soul is crushed with grief to the point of death. Stay here and keep watch with me." He went on a little farther and fell to the ground…Then he returned and found the disciples asleep. He said to Peter, "Simon, are you asleep? Couldn't you watch with me even one hour?" (Mark 14:33-37).

You'd think Peter would have caught on that something awful was about to happen and he'd respond by keeping alert. But no. He was human, more prone to doing wrong than right.

Three times Jesus returned to find all three sacked out, heads on rocks, breaching the garden's sanctity with their snores.

Then without warning, torches blazed before them as a crowd of men approached, wielding clubs and swords. Peter finally rose to the occasion in a hotheaded blur. Suddenly eager to defend Jesus, he drew his sword and slashed off the ear of the high priest's slave.

Picture the fury of tempers flaring as Jesus, the constant comforter, faced his greatest hour of need. In return for the love he showed his disciples, they caved in to their fears and fled, deserting him.

And then came Peter's lowest moments. As Jesus predicted, that night Peter was confronted three times for being seen with him. Three times Peter denied ever knowing him.

The next day Peter watched armed soldiers batter Jesus mercilessly, saw blood course down the Messiah's gentle face. He knew the depth of his betrayal and the regret of his actions. And he knew he could never take back what he had done.

I can almost hear Peter's heart echo frantically from the well of regret during those first minutes of realization, and I catch myself feeling thankful that *I* did not mess up so hugely. My relief is far too short-lived for my preference, though, because it doesn't take long to remember how often I've been guilty of the same sins of arrogance and betrayal. Peter's story reminds me that I'd be in big trouble if God didn't offer me the lifeline of redemption. I'd be stuck in that dried-up pit otherwise.

Peter lived to experience God's redemption in a mighty way, and I can too every day of my life. This truth opens the floodgates in my spirit and refreshes me with my Savior's grace.

Before Jesus died, he declared, " 'You are blessed, Simon son of John, because my Father in heaven has revealed this to you…Now I say to you that you are Peter (which means 'rock'), and upon this rock I will build my church, and all the powers of hell will not conquer it. And I will give you the keys of the Kingdom of Heaven" (Matthew 16:17-19).

When Peter finally got it, he got it. The king of impulsiveness grew into a rock-solid hero of faith. Through his mistakes, he learned true strength. He understood firsthand the power of each decision and the cost of regret. However, he didn't wallow in his shame, but moved forward in God's mercy to become a founder of the early church. He took the message of God's love to the Jewish people similarly to how the apostle Paul did to the rest of the world.

This man who denied knowing Jesus, who acted without thinking and ran when his fears got the best of him, was executed for his faith and reputedly chose to hang upside down on a cross because he wasn't worthy to die as his Savior did.

One of my favorite qualities about God is his love of redemption. That might seem like a "Well, duh" statement, but I've been a Christian so long that sometimes I have to stop and think about the breadth of God's goodness. Like forgetful Peter, who couldn't stay alert and couldn't manage to acknowledge his Lord, it's easy for me to take Jesus for granted.

How does God feel about our regrets? Well, it's more than amazing that he not only forgives us for our screwups, but he also loves to be an overachiever and bring *good* from them. As if saving us weren't enough.

Check out some phrases Webster's dictionary uses to define the word *redeem*: to buy back; to win back; to free from what distresses or harms; to free from captivity by payment of ransom; to help to overcome something detrimental; to release from blame or debt; to change for the better; to offset the bad effect of; reform, repair, restore.[1]

If you haven't gotten excited about this before, it's time. Look closely at those words: *win, free from what distresses, overcome, release from blame…*

God sees you as worth fighting for. To "win" implies there's a prize involved. That prize is you, and God went to extreme lengths to win you back.

God's redemption extends further than his greatest act of offering us eternal life through Jesus' death. In turning the negatives into positives, our heavenly Father shows that he cares utterly about our quality of life on earth. He uses our failings to bring us closer to himself and to reveal his power to change lives. We still have to deal with consequences of our decisions, but our hearts don't have to stay thirsty because of them.

How far will you let God take you beyond the decisions of your past? Oftentimes we remain captive to the same old worn-out accusations that run through our heads. We feel that somehow living with ongoing guilt is like penance we deserve to pay.

But our debt died on the cross with Jesus, and our freedom from blame came alive along with him.

So how does God feel about your regrets? He feels like redeeming them. He feels like rehydrating your spirit and bringing you to a place of victory for the rest of your life, strong and vital to make a difference for him.

You are more to God than the quality of your decisions and the acts of your past. Now, faced with that potential, move forward and leave the draining regrets behind. They belong in the pit. You do not. So take hold of the lifeline God holds down to you, and climb on out.

*This is what the LORD says—your Redeemer, the Holy
One of Israel:..."I am the LORD, your Holy One, Israel's
Creator, your King." This is what the LORD says—he
who made a way through the sea, a path through the
mighty waters..."Forget the former things; do not
dwell on the past. See, I am doing a new thing! Now it
springs up; do you not perceive it? I am making a way
in the desert and streams in the wasteland...I provide
water in the desert and streams in the wasteland,
to give drink to my people, my chosen, the people I
formed for myself that they may proclaim my praise."*

ISAIAH 43:14-21 NIV

CONSIDER THIS...

1. Most likely you can think of several people whose lives have been altered by decisions that seemed small. How might their lives be different now if it weren't for those actions? Looking back, can you remember a close call when you nearly changed the course of your life and are now thankful you didn't? Have you made any shortsighted decisions you're still paying for?

2. Do you struggle to believe that God can bring good out of your mistakes, big or small? If you could ask him for any redo, what would your request involve? What would you like to see God do to redeem a past error?

3. Read Job 19, particularly verses 25-27. Job was a man who lived for God, yet he went through a horrendous season when God allowed his faith to be tested. His friends criticized him, and his wife even told him to curse God and die in order to be free of his

torment. Although her advice was wrong, surely she spoke out of love for him because she ached to see him in such pain. Yet Job hung in there in faith, and God redeemed his life, going so far as to bless him with more than Job had lost. What might some costs have been had Job followed his wife's advice and given up hope in God? What messed and missed opportunities might Job have faced? Had Job's faith been weaker, as Peter's was early on, what regrets may he have dealt with?

4. Psalm 19:14 is a great verse to pray every day, considering how many words come out of our mouths and how easily our attitudes can pull us into regrettable decisions. This verse also involves the idea of God as our rock and redeemer. Think creatively: What are some characteristics of a rock that tie into the idea of the power of redemption? Why would the psalmist find comfort in God as both his rock and redeemer? What insights does this offer you about redemption? (See also Psalm 78:35.)

5. Isaiah 54:8 is another great verse that describes some of God's emotions surrounding our mistakes. Read through the entire chapter and think about what your mistakes and sins cost God. It's easy to forget that each sin cost Jesus his life. Each one. Knowing your particular set of sins, think through a few that bring the most shame to your heart. God redeemed that one, and that one…and that one too. In view of Isaiah 54, how do you think God feels about your regrets? Pray through your thoughts, and ask him to help you feel his heart regarding your past.

16

SHED THE STINK
OF UNFORGIVENESS.

His head began to clear as the smell hit him. Although he couldn't see anything, he knew he didn't want to be there—wherever there was.

He gagged once, twice, then vomited into the slop that sloshed around his wrists and ankles. He shook his head and tried to clear the blackness and fear, but they engulfed him.

Where was he?

He dared to feel around him. Slime covered the walls of his cave... was it a cave?

More awake, he searched his subconscious for something familiar, a memory, any clue to this prison.

Around him, sounds of groaning and churning muffled together. Self-protection pressed him back toward the wall, where he pulled his knees into his chest and willed himself to breathe past the odor.

His gut roiled again at the stench, and he vomited once more. The pain in his head thudded down to his shoulders. His stomach gurgled, but the idea of food made him gag.

Time passed, but in this foul liquid world he had no sense of hours or days.

Images flashed. A boat. Sailors. The storm.

Yes, he had been on a ship. Going…his head throbbed…going any place that wasn't Nineveh.

With that thought, the whole picture cleared, even though he remained in the dark.

He had been running from God. Running in the opposite direction from Nineveh, where God had told him to go.

Those people didn't deserve God's forgiveness.

And now look, he was paying for it. For *their* sins.

If few things are as draining as a big old regret, just as few hold us captive as powerfully as unforgiveness.

I am a Jonah. I have been trapped by the foulness of a self-righteous, unforgiving attitude. Unfortunately, there really was no running from it. However, the upside to not being able to escape something is being forced to deal with it.

Do you know Jonah's story? God chose him to warn the Ninevite people to repent. Nineveh was the capital of Assyria, an evil empire that had dealt countless atrocities to Israel. Dreading that God would show mercy to such heinous people if they did repent, Jonah ran in the other direction. He hopped on a ship headed west, hoping to outrun God's command.

You can guess how that went over with God. He sent a fierce storm to capsize the ship. In order to save the rest of the sailors' lives, Jonah told them to throw him overboard. At least he knew he'd caused the trouble. With compassionate discipline, and a sense of humor, God sent an enormous fish to swallow the wayward prophet. Three days later, the creature spit Jonah onto the land, and onward to Nineveh Jonah went. In the between time, Jonah had lots of food for thought, even if it was half digested.

Jonah did all he could to hang on to his self-righteousness, but God is one creative Being. He comes up with an endless array of strategies to refine our character.

Given how I can relate to Jonah, I oughta be super grateful I haven't wound up in the belly of a fish as a godly time-out to think about what I've done.

I wonder how long Jonah spent there before he grasped the irony of his lesson. The Ninevites, whom he believed weren't worthy of forgiveness, slept safely in their beds while he, God's prophet, was subjected to three days in vile seclusion wading through a fish's digestive system.

I didn't grasp the breadth of it myself until several years ago when I woke up to smell the stink of my own self-righteousness.

Sure, being inside a fish's stomach would have been terrifying, but let's not miss God's bigger point: It's more terrifying to face God's anger. The fish was an act of mercy on God's part. Although Jonah did not want to show a forgiving attitude toward his enemies, God showed Jonah gracious forgiveness for his self-righteousness.

Forgiveness has never come easily for me. For Jonah and me, I think our problems with this virtue tie into 1) an unhealthy need for control and 2) a distorted view of our own goodness.

God made it very clear to Jonah who was in the wrong, and shock of all shocks, it was Jonah more so than the dreaded Ninevites.

Like Jonah, I've come to understand my need for grace a whole lot more. In the past, my self-righteousness hurt a couple of friendships, and to this day I carry regrets about things I said and did. But God wants to bring good from our mistakes. I hope each day I'm inviting him to do just that.

The struggle to forgive is universal. The reasons why are probably endless, but maybe it's because when we've been hurt by someone, we feel something has been stolen from us. The thought of offering forgiveness feels as if we're giving that person more of ourselves that they don't deserve. It's an understandable rationalization, but as with so many of God's ways, he sees things differently.

Another reason we might be reluctant to forgive is because we're afraid to give up control. When something has been taken from us, whatever the form of the hurt, we feel a loss of control; someone breached our protective walls. To compensate, we clamor for any shred of control. Refusing to forgive fools us into thinking we've regained some of it.

In actuality, when we choose to hold a grudge, we continue to place ourselves in the position of victim, not victor. And we're guilty of sinning on top of it.

Jonah's eyes were finally opened in that dark prison at sea. He had no idea whether he'd make it out alive, but he turned to God before it was too late:

> "When my life had almost gone, I remembered the LORD. I prayed to you, and you heard my prayers in your Holy Temple. People who worship useless idols give up their loyalty to you. But I will praise and thank you while I give sacrifices to you, and I will keep my promises to you. Salvation comes from the LORD!" Then the LORD spoke to the fish, and the fish threw up Jonah onto the dry land (Jonah 2:7-10 NCV).

Yesterday I had a belly-of-the-fish experience. I call it that because it gave me a glimpse of God's view of forgiveness.

Steve and I took Paxton to church for the first time. With Easter a few weeks away, the service focused on the cross. We had not been to church for the past few weeks while we'd been ensconced at home with our newborn, so both of us were craving that time of worship. It was especially meaningful to be there as a family, and I think our emotions were primed for a big dose of God's voice speaking to us.

The music and the message revolved around Jesus' sacrifice and how easy it is to forget the importance of the wonderful, awful cross that was God's chosen method of winning us back to himself.

Throughout the service I looked over at my sleeping baby in my husband's arms and couldn't stop the tears. I've already said it's easy for me to take for granted my need for God's forgiveness. But my little one…he would be going to hell if God didn't love him enough to send his Son to die for Paxton Elijah Marshall. My precious child would suffer for eternity if Jesus hadn't prized him above his own life, if he hadn't chosen to release his right to a grudge.

When the service was over and the lights went up, I saw Steve wiping his own tears. Obviously he'd had a moment too.

As we were driving away, I told him about my new perspective being there with Pax.

Steve nodded.

"Sometimes I forget what it cost God to save me," I said. "But looking at Pax made me realize what his future would be if Jesus hadn't died for him."

Steve looked at me, eyes rimmed with moisture. "And to think about sacrificing him for the rest of the world—" He shook his head to cast off the unthinkable.

No way. There's absofreakinlutely no way I'd do it.

Steve glanced in the rearview mirror at his son. One father's heart understanding Another's.

I don't often consider the devastation my sin cost my heavenly Father. I neglect to realize that a heart as big as God's, that feels love as big as God's does, also has the capacity to feel incredible hurt.

Who am I to think that sending his precious Son to die didn't tear God's heart out? It absolutely did. *I* tore God's heart out.

But he doesn't hold a grudge against me. He forgave me. And he's preparing an amazing future for me forever with him. He not only let go of his right to hold my sin against me, but he wants to be with me forever.

That's forgiveness. Because he freely offered it, I'm free to accept it.

Forgiveness carries unlimited potential for healing, and with healing comes freedom. But it doesn't ordinarily come easily for us.

It didn't for Jonah. After three days bound up in a fish, he still fought his desire to carry a grudge against the Ninevites, even after they turned to God. Once the fish spat him out, he was free—or was he?

We'll constantly face reasons to hold on to our anger and nurse our hurts, but we'll be the ones in the wrong, and we'll continue to suffer those hurts when we don't deal with them.

Knowing all that is old hat for me, sad to say. But yesterday God gave me fresh awareness of it through an unexpected hour at church.

I hope your day brings you the sweetness of God's forgiveness, and a belly-of-the-fish moment designed especially for you by the God who designed his plan of forgiveness especially for you.

Forgive one another as quickly and thoroughly as God in Christ forgave you.

EPHESIANS 4:32 MSG

CONSIDER THIS...

1. Getting right to the point, is there anyone you're holding a grudge against? What happened between you and that person? Is he or she aware of your feelings? Why do you think it's been so hard to forgive?

2. How deeply have you thought about what it cost God to forgive you? Considering it now, how do you feel knowing God can be hurt? How does that knowledge affect your attitude about forgiving others? Which do you think is more difficult, being the forgiver or the forgiven? Why?

3. Developing a forgiving spirit doesn't come naturally to most people. It takes a work of God's Spirit to change the heart from the inside. How do these verses help you keep his voice fresh in your mind to strengthen you to forgive? Psalm 25:7,11; 86:5; Mark 11:24-25; Luke 6:37-38; Ephesians 4:32. Instead of burying

your feelings, how might you proactively work toward growing a forgiving spirit?

4. Matthew 6:9-15 is the Lord's Prayer, which includes a line asking God to forgive us as we forgive others. Based on your usual willingness to forgive, how much do you think God will forgive you?

5. Read Matthew 18:21-35. Verse 22 speaks about how much we're to forgive, up to seventy times seven. Since most people wouldn't keep track of each time they forgive, what do you think Jesus' basic point is? Does this passage reassure you or scare you? Why?

RELAX AND TAKE
A LOAD OFF.

As I type, Paxton is fighting sleep. Snuggled against me in his BabyBjörn carrier, he looks up every couple of minutes with a wail that gradually gentles with each wave of crying. Shorter and shorter these outbursts last, each one followed by a soft thud as his head rests again on my chest.

Sweetly pathetic.

His eyes droop, tiny mouth curls in a precious pout.

"Give it up, buddy," I whisper and cuddle him closer.

If he'd only let rest claim him, he'd be so much more comfortable.

A tender four weeks old today, he doesn't yet know how to find sleep. It just sort of finds him each time he's too tired to stay awake. Steve and I know the health of his whole little being depends on the regularity of his sleep patterns, and we've been studying parenting books in order to guide him to the rest he needs.

Lemme tell you, it's a challenge. We didn't get it till we got it. We had heard about the 24/7 demands of life with a newborn, but experiencing it for the first time has provided some of the only clarity our foggy brains can understand these days on so few hours of slumber. We get how chronic busyness without adequate breaks can mess with a body.

What busyness does a newborn have? Plenty! Every time he opens his eyes, he's inundated with stimuli he has to learn to process. It's every bit the hard work grown-ups do, modified for size. He can't handle adult-sized stresses, but he has a big load to bear with his current job description: Newborn on the grow!

The current priority of sleep in our house reminds me of God's wisdom when it comes to our need for rest. I understand more now why God set up a Sabbath rest and told us to stick to it.

How grossly I overlooked it before, when I felt it was optional. But wear me out long enough, and every cell in me craves a Sabbath rest *right now.* And how about one tomorrow too?

Why do we fight what's good for us? I'm a bundle of excuses when it comes to prioritizing downtime. I love the idea in theory—amen, hallelujah—but I don't often practice Sabbath rest as seriously as I should.

I usually chase after more drivenness at the expense of rest. Programmed by a so-called need to get things done, I think of relaxing as a cop-out when there are still things to cross off my to-do list. Oftentimes it takes more effort to slow down than it does to continue running at a frenetic pace.

In the far recesses of my psyche, I do yearn for a break, so in futile hopes of "finishing," I compensate by trying to do many things at once. Multitasking is one of my favorite pastimes, and I usually practice it with flourish.

Anyone relate?

There aren't many moments in the day when I'm doing fewer than two things at once. Take right now, for instance…writing a book and soothing my child. If you peeked in my house on other days, you might find me editing, checking e-mail, visiting blogs, returning phone calls, preparing meals, eating, cleaning house, exercising, reading— amazing how many tasks can be done simultaneously.

Truth be told, I realize my penchant for many projects gets in the way of slowing my brain and giving it time to catch up. After a while, I end up distracted and frazzled because I don't have a sense of excellence or fulfillment from focusing on only one thing and knowing I've done my best. I begin to feel as if life is edging away from me, and I'm run ragged by everything I've put above spending time in Sabbath rest.

I've always thought of Sabbath rest as an ancient concept that couldn't possibly fit in today's hyperbusy world. But what does it take to make me realize God knows I need rest so badly that he included it in his Ten Commandments? Hello? How much clearer could he spell it out?

It's right there in black-and-white. Exodus 20:8-10 says, "Remember the Sabbath by keeping it holy. Six days you shall labor and do all your work, but the seventh day is a Sabbath to the LORD your God. On it you shall not do any work" (NIV). And Leviticus 16:31 refers to "a Sabbath day of complete rest for you."

Sabbath rest was (and is) so important to God that he even called for the land to rest (Leviticus 26:34). He instructed his people, the Israelites, to follow his Sabbath rules to a T, with dire consequences for those who didn't (Leviticus 23:30-31).

When did God initiate the Sabbath rest? Actually, he practiced it himself first, way back after creation: "On the seventh day God had finished his work of creation, so he rested from all his work. And God blessed the seventh day and declared it holy, because it was the day when he rested from all his work of creation" (Genesis 2:2-3).

Three things about these verses:

First, I mentioned that I'm full of excuses for why I need to attend to the next thing, and the next, and the next. But my excuses continue to bring me back to the fact that even God rested, so how much more do we humans need it?

Second, I knew God took a break after he finished his work, but notice that God *finished* creating everything.

Enter Excuse No. 1. My trouble with taking breaks usually comes because there's always something more to do. I never feel finished. Sure, I complete projects, but there's always one waiting in the wings demanding my attention. Well, that excuse tanks pretty fast. As if God doesn't have bunches of projects going on at once. He's more of a multitasker than all of us combined.

The third point I notice in these verses is that rest is holy. Now, that thought strikes me as wrong, even though it has to be true since it's right there in the Bible. It's just that sitting around doing nothing flies in the face of my Type A personality. I don't like being bored, and if there's one thing I can't stand at the end of the day, it's feeling like I've accomplished nothing. (There you have Excuses 2 and 3.)

However, Sabbath rest is not doing nothing. There isn't anything boring or lazy about the downtime God commands us to take. His rest is rejuvenating, like a loofah sponge that invigorates at the same time it soothes.

Ahh...feel the relief.

I can—no, I *should*—take time-outs to relax for the holiness aspect alone. Rest brings me to a quiet place where I can hear God's voice. Separated from the din of the day, I'm more able to process what he's saying to me. I'm also more open to becoming like him.

In order to appreciate the Sabbath's nonnegotiable value, we need to understand God's purpose for it. He set it up as a time for us to focus on him, to gather with his other followers, and to be refreshed from our work (Deuteronomy 5:12-15).

God set up regular weekly Sabbaths as well as special ones during festivals and certain years (Leviticus 23; 25:1-22), so a sabbath doesn't only mean a church day on Sunday. It can be any time specifically set aside for God, for other Christians, and for R&R.

Sounds great! Surely we can fit all that into scattered time slots throughout the week, right?

Possibly. That is, if there's a conscious effort made. All God's instructions make me think he wants more than a hit-or-miss approach to Sabbath rest, lest it get lost in the other stuff of life. He knows how easily this overlooked Commandment gets buried at the bottom of the in-box or under piles of laundry, and the cost of missing out on it is too high.

You see, there's more to the Sabbath than what it does for us. Superseding what we get out of it, God cherishes his Sabbath because he intends that we spend some of it with him. Isaiah 58:13-14 explains this:

> Keep the Sabbath day holy. Don't pursue your own inter-ests on that day, but enjoy the Sabbath and speak of it with delight as the LORD's holy day. Honor the Sabbath in everything you do on that day, and don't follow your own desires or talk idly. Then the LORD will be your delight.

When we don't stop to consider our spiritual priorities regarding our time, our priorities typically steer us onto selfish paths where our agenda instead of God's becomes the focus.

It's about God and us together. He values our rest not only as a way to honor him, but as a preventive measure to ward off burnout, depression, ineffectiveness, and sickness.

Most people I know tend to overbook, overplan, and overdo until they're overdone. Because our society values us for our accomplish-ments, many of us become enslaved to the ugly side of drivenness.

Just for kicks, take a look at the past few weeks in your planner. Is there much white space left each day amid the reminders you have jotted down? Perhaps you're even one of those people who writes down what you have already done because you love the thrill of crossing things off.

It's as if we enjoy defying the limits of a 24-hour day. By the time we reach our midtwenties, most of us know the drain of pulling an all-nighter. Whatever we cram into those late-night hours—homework, housework, socializing, career pursuits—the majority of twentysome-things are on their way to mastering the dubious skill of *overdoing* to the point of *overlooking* the long-term effects of neglecting rest. It would seem God knew in advance that we'd turn out to be a bunch of stressed-out folks who don't stop when we ought to.

God takes his call for rest seriously, regardless of whether we do. If we don't heed his warnings about making time to relax, he may allow other detours to slow us down. Those aren't fun when they take the form of health troubles and relationship problems. Sometimes he uses creative time-outs to realign our wheels on his healthier track.

Many places in the Bible speak about God offering rest to us, providing us with peace, refreshing our spirits. Psalm 23, for starters. These six verses are loaded with wonderful imagery that makes me want to curl up in a heavenly hammock and lounge the day away with my Savior:

> The LORD is my shepherd, I shall not be in want. He makes me lie down in green pastures, he leads me beside quiet waters, he restores my soul. He guides me in paths of righteousness...Your rod and your staff, they comfort me. You prepare a table before me...You anoint my head with oil; my cup overflows. Surely goodness and love will follow me all the days of my life, and I will dwell in the house of the LORD forever (NIV).

From lying down in green pastures and being led beside quiet waters, God loves when we take time for soul restoration and the pursuit of righteousness (becoming more like him). Other images about being comforted, feasting, overflowing with God's goodness and love, and dwelling at home with God ease our overstimulated senses with his calming presence.

Notice, though, that God has to *make* us lie down in green pastures. The human condition requires God's gentle pressure at times to get us to a place of rest.

Sort of like young Pax learning how to find sleep. He needs our guidance. But when he finally gives in, serenity shows all over his face and body, and he becomes a cuddly picture of peace. I see myself in him. In my own ways I fight God's guiding touch as he leads me to rest.

I came across some verses a while back that hit between the eyes.

I had read them many times, but this wording caught me off guard with its appeal:

> Are you tired? Worn out?...Come to me. Get away with me and you'll recover your life. I'll show you how to take a real rest. Walk with me and work with me—watch how I do it. Learn the unforced rhythms of grace. I won't lay anything heavy or ill-fitting on you. Keep company with me and you'll learn to live freely and lightly (Matthew 11:28-30 MSG).

Isn't that beautiful? I need to "learn the unforced rhythms of grace."

By practicing them, we set ourselves up for a life rich with fulfillment and purpose. God won't have to *make* us lie down in green pastures. We'll curl ourselves up near him and listen to him whisper words of peace and rest.

That will be a true Sabbath if I've ever experienced one.

Those who live in the shelter of the Most High
will find rest in the shadow of the Almighty.

PSALM 91:1

CONSIDER THIS...

1. Does rest come easily for you? What are your favorite forms of relaxation? What typically puts you in a restful mood? What prevents you from resting? What do you think a good balance between work and rest looks like?

2. In your own words, contrast laziness with rest. Consider how a verse such as Psalm 127:2, which says, "It is vain for you to rise

up early, to take rest late, to eat the bread of [anxious] toil—for He gives [blessings] to His beloved in sleep" (AMP) coincides with one like Proverbs 13:4, which says, "Lazy people want much but get little, but those who work hard will prosper." How is a lazy person not necessarily resting as God intends for Sabbath rest? When speaking of Sabbath rest, how is doing nothing actually very productive? What does Sabbath rest produce?

3. It's ironic that God, who needs no rest, made time for it. (And him with a never-ending to-do list!) His example shows clearly the importance of downtime. Check out these verses for more about God (Jesus) at rest. Several times he escaped the press of the crowd to get away for quiet time (Mark 4:35-36; 6:30-32). Mark 4:35-41 tells the story of Jesus calming a storm at sea. His disciples got in a tizzy because he slept while they feared for their lives. In response, he asked them about the quality of their faith. How might a person's connection to (or faith in) Jesus affect his or her perspective on making time for rest?

4. The Pharisees criticized Jesus for working on the Sabbath (Luke 13:10-17). Summarize Jesus' response. What wisdom does his response give you regarding a balance of rest and work?

5. A Christian's ultimate rest will be in eternity. It's interesting that the Bible refers to heaven as a place of rest, not one filled with to-do lists (Hebrews 4:1-11). Point made? How do you picture God's rest in heaven? For more on rest that God offers, take a look at these verses: Psalm 4:8; 116:7; 127:2.

LEND A HAND AND HELP YOURSELF.

I saw the most precious thing this week. Living outside town, we see a lot of wildlife pass through our yard. One of my favorite sightings is a group of deer that meander down to the lake. Depending on the season, I can spot them morning or late afternoon from my office window, often several times a week.

I hadn't seen them for a while, though, because my routine with a little one at home has drastically shifted. However, a window above the changing table in Paxton's room looks out over the woodpile and a stand of pine trees, where I caught a glimpse the other day while changing a diaper.

Chatting to my baby, I glanced up and my heart skipped at the sweetest vision of another mama with her new child. I'd never seen a younger fawn except in pictures. From 20 yards away I could see every spot on its tawny coat and every wobble of its tiny legs. Heartstopper moment.

I must still be purging pregnancy hormones because a lump clogged my throat and my eyes filled with tears. "Look, Pax," I said. "Look at the little deer, babe!"

He continued his new trick of showing me his tongue.

I giggled and kissed his tummy, then looked again at the other mother-child pair out the window. The doe moved through the trees, and the baby tripped keeping up with her. Its legs gave out, and it went kerplunk, flat on its belly on the ground. With what appeared to be a sigh of resignation, the fawn plopped its head on its front hooves and lay there for a couple of seconds, as if to ask the world what a guy had to do to get some help around here. It's tough to be little.

Welcome to earth, sweet thing.

Haven't we all been there? Flat on our faces, we feel small and vulnerable to the toughness of life. Any willing hand of help is like a rush of cool water on a thirsty throat or a mama's loving nudge to get us back on our feet.

We all need help to stand tall and walk strong. And we all need to be available to offer a nudge for someone else.

Spring has sprung in northwest Arkansas, and with it comes a plethora of insights from nature. It occurred to me as I replayed the scene of the deer that God even designed animals to live in community. They need to connect with their own kind, to give and accept help from each other.

How much more so do we humans need one another.

I've run the gamut from wanting to do everything on my own to wishing for more community, and from being Volunteer No. 1 to hoping no one would ask me for another thing. But no matter what my current frame of mind, I can't get away from the fact that we're created to need other people.

Until recent years I didn't take to heart my responsibility to be available to the point that it cost me much. I've said before that I was spoiled with my time for many years. I'd help when it was convenient for me or when I wanted a notch in the do-gooder spot in my subconscious.

Maybe that sounds exaggerated, and maybe it is. Of course there are lots of times when I'm happy to help out. My point is that there always has been a strain of selfishness in me when it comes to giving until it hurts. I'd smile benignly at the oft-heard phrase that it's better to give than to receive (Acts 20:35), but inside I'd cringe lest anyone ask me to give too much. I had my schedule to keep, you know.

Okay, truth time. I still haven't become a pro at the giving thing. I look at volunteers at church who faithfully show up every week to direct traffic or serve in the nursery, and I think *every* week? I know I was not given the spiritual gift of helps. I know because it makes me glad not to have received it. If I had it, I'd love it. How twisted am I.

I can say that I have made progress, however little that counts. I realize one key element of living for God and of maintaining balance (a topic we'll get to later) revolves around paying attention to others' needs. Making the sacrifice to help others brings healthy Christian living full circle and refuels the giver, although it can seem like a paradox for someone with a weary soul and parched energy reserves.

Jesus loved a good paradox. Did you know he's the one responsible for that "more blessed to give than to receive" phrase? He knows how selfish humans are, because at the crux of his words lies an appeal to how we're wired—to think of ourselves. Yeah, we want more blessings! Bring 'em on.

Lest we bend his intention the wrong way, though, we can bet he didn't give us the phrase as an excuse to keep putting ourselves first. He meant for us to focus on the giving part and let the receiving part come as an afterthought.

That said, let's think about what helping others does in our own lives. Helping others takes the mind off personal troubles, honors God, and actually refills an empty heart-tank. Selfishness in regard to time and love not only starves others who need it, but it also dries out the person who withholds it. It prevents a person from realizing the benefits of community and God's sufficiency in weakness.

Part of my unhelpful attitude stems from failing to cherish the gift of community. This thought struck me two mornings ago when

I was up before light. The stars out the kitchen window twinkled against the night sky, and I realized I hadn't noticed them in a long time. Typically caught up in the immediate, I neglect to pause long enough to remember they exist, much less to enjoy their beauty. But in the morning's quiet moments, I was blessed by them.

Isn't that how it is with people? We grow accustomed to their presence to the point that we forget to pay them real mind. We forget there's a vulnerable heart in each one. Like fixtures, they are always in the background. It's the worst with those closest to us.

When I remember how blessed I am to have people around me, I feel a natural outpouring of desire to be there for them, even strangers whose stories I know nothing about. We're in this life thing together, and we cheat ourselves as well as others when we fail to dive in and make helping a basic part of our days. It should be a given, not up for discussion. But I've deserved a boot to the behind many times for groaning over "interruptions" to my oh-so-precious hours.

The human heart is fragile, much like that tiny fawn. No matter how someone hides it, there's still a tender five-year-old inside the most weathered adult. We all need to be noticed, to be seen and cared for, and we leave a wake of emotional carnage behind us when we lack the sensitivity to defend the heart of someone who needs us. That's a tragedy, made even worse when we don't see it as such.

I've been guilty of this when it comes to my parents. They've been givers to me my entire life, but as I moved through my twenties I began to understand more deeply that they have needs and emotions I've taken for granted.

I also think of how often I've shown little patience for a telemarketer or a slow driver or the store clerk who spends extra moments chatting with another customer. I'm ashamed at my tendency to opt for a critical attitude instead of seeking to understand and add delight to someone's day. I wish I'd spent more of my twenties transitioning from expecting help to becoming a helper. But I'm learning to remember the overwhelming amount of pain in the world, because I don't want to compound another's hurt by failing to care for their heart. I want other hearts to be more full through their contact with mine.

You know the story of the Good Samaritan. He's the guy Jesus told about in Luke 10:25-37 who stopped to help a man who'd been beaten, robbed, and left for dead. Simple enough, but there are twists that make it extra interesting. For one, Samaritans were looked down on by the Jews. And this guy stopped to help after a Jewish priest and a Levite passed on by, ignoring one of their own. In fact, he went beyond the call of duty by taking the man to an inn where he cared for the man's wounds. He also paid the innkeeper to see to the man's needs the next day and offered to foot the bill if additional care was needed.

Jesus told the story in response to a Jewish religious expert's question about just how far he had to go for others. He asked who his neighbor was, prompting Jesus' reply about the Samaritan who gave until it hurt—although the Samaritan's heart seemed to be generous enough that giving didn't hurt.

Hmm. Maybe that's a key point. Mother Teresa said of this, "I have found the paradox that if I love until it hurts, then there is no hurt, but only more love."

Martin Luther King Jr. voiced an amazing insight about the story of the Good Samaritan. He said, "The first question which the priest and the Levite asked was: 'If I stop to help this man, what will happen to me?' But...the good Samaritan reversed the question: 'If I do not stop to help this man, what will happen to him?' "

One of the most convicting verses in the Bible for me is Mark 10:45, when Jesus said, "Even the Son of Man did not come to be served, but to serve, and to give his life as a ransom for many" (NIV).

Jesus came to serve us. What in the world was he thinking? He's God, the King and Master of the universe. Yet he keeps giving to *me* despite my sinful status as a human and my unappealing me-first motivations.

I'm not sure what to do with that. It's more than mind bending. I'm not sure I'll ever get it, even when I can ask him about it face-to-face someday.

I've got to ask myself, though, if I'm applying his heart to my actions more each year. Am I more willing to give of myself now than I was a year ago? My answer to that question reveals a lot about my growing maturity as a Christian.

Yeah, that doesn't always sit well with me—another smack of conviction right in the face. But what a beautiful countenance I'll have someday when my face finally reveals Jesus' serving heart in me as second nature instead of second thought. I thank the Lord every day that he isn't done with me. (I can picture my loved ones nodding their heads in agreement!)

Giving hurts only when the heart isn't complete, and our hearts won't be finished until we're with Jesus for eternity. Until then, may we experience the treasured pain of putting others first.

And may we be blessed with growth and depth in return.

The righteous give generously.

Psalm 37:21 niv

CONSIDER THIS...

1. We don't get to pick our spiritual gifts, those skills and passions God gives us to help show his love to others. But if you could pick yours, would the gift of helps be one you'd choose? Why or why not?

2. Are you one who typically jumps up and offers your time and resources for someone else? Looking more at motivations, when you do help, what prompts you? Are you motivated because you want to make someone's life easier? Because you want to feel like a good person? A mix of reasons? What thoughts cross your mind when you consider that God sees your true motivations, even ones you don't know exist?

3. Second Timothy 2:20-21 (MSG) says, "In a well-furnished kitchen there are not only crystal goblets and silver platters, but waste cans and compost buckets—some containers used to serve fine meals, others to take out the garbage. Become the kind of container God can use to present any and every kind of gift to his guests for their blessing." What characteristics are necessary to be useful to God?

4. What assurance does Hebrews 6:10 offer about your acts of service here on earth? How does focusing on eternity boost your desire to serve others now?

5. First Thessalonians 5:13-15 (MSG) says, "Get along among yourselves, each of you doing your part...Reach out for the exhausted, pulling them to their feet. Be patient with each person, attentive to individual needs. And be careful that when you get on each other's nerves you don't snap at each other. Look for the best in each other, and always do your best to bring it out." The Good Samaritan may have looked for the best in the man he stopped to help. How can our nurturing acts of help bring out the best in someone else? What power does positive reinforcement have in relationships?

19

BALANCE IS NOT JUST FOR GYMNASTS.

I was going to be a world-class gymnast.

It's true. On my way to becoming an Olympic figure skater, I planned to earn a gold on the balance beam. After that, I'd take up water ballet and then top off my career with an encore in gymnastics, only that time around it would be rhythmic.

Since my gymnastics training was short lived and I never took an ice-skating lesson, maybe all that will happen in my heavenly life. This life has not taken me down the road of championship athletics, which is probably good considering how tough it would have been to balance all those talents (grin). And I'm all about balance. I was going to medal on the beam, remember. Got to stay steady for that.

Balance is the glue that keeps a gymnast on the beam, just like it's the stuff that keeps the parts of life together. Without it, a person comes unglued.

Balance is one of my favorite words. I like the sound of it and the concept even better. Just enough work, just enough play. A bit of socializing, a dose of alone time. Balanced diet, balanced checkbook, balanced brain. It's all good.

The older I get, the more responsibilities accumulate, and the more

I realize how much training (and good coaching) it takes to keep up a balanced life.

What part of life doesn't need balance? Take our relationships. We've got to know how to help and be helped. When to say yes and when to put up boundaries. How to recognize a healthy boundary from a rigid emotional wall, and how to appreciate balance in others.

Then there's the spiritual side. How does one uphold God's standards without becoming judgmental? Or how do we learn to accept ourselves as we are—as God does—all the while seeking to become more like him? And how do we balance the earthly with the spiritual? As Christians, we're living *on* earth but *for* heaven. Talk about conflicting interests.

No one told me when I entered adulthood that establishing a balanced life would be such a workout, requiring strength, flexibility, and endurance. Finding balance is like that gold medal hanging just beyond my reach. All I want is to grab it and hang it in a display case, sealed forever where it can't escape.

I may be harping on an issue that doesn't seem super important to you. If you've never felt the effects of living completely out of sync, then you might not appreciate the value of balance. Imbalance isn't always easy to spot in ourselves until its negative effects start showing up repeatedly. Then we wonder why life isn't working so smoothly anymore.

For instance, it's tough to put the brakes on habitually saying yes to long hours at work when you have a goal to keep climbing the ladder. It's also tough to start saying no to someone you love who needs a lot of emotional support when you're always expected to provide it. It's hard to stop the push toward excess of anything, but there has to be balance to our *yeses* and *nos* if we're going to stay healthy for the long haul.

I learned this lesson in my early twenties when I was working so much and living so little. However, I've said before that I'm a bit dense. I seem to return frequently to the point of burnout after I take on too much or fail to be true to my emotional limits or allow one area of life to monopolize the others.

You've seen gymnasts flip over the uneven parallel bars, right? That's me unglued. Spinning in circles, getting nowhere but dizzy. When I'm living in upheaval from putting too much energy into one thing, my perspectives become skewed, and I get nauseated by emotions that can't remain steady for all the ups and downs. Desperate for relief, I succumb to a couple of pressures. First, to despair about the future. And second, to push harder to prove that my life is worthwhile.

Back when I experienced the worst of this—right out of college when I was working three jobs that left no time for rest or fun—I began to see my future as a hopeless cycle of exhaustion, lacking joy and peace. I felt as if I were glued to the high bar, catching brief glimpses of everyone else enjoying normal lives. But I couldn't relate because I never slowed the chaos enough to get my feet on the ground and return order to life. I couldn't understand why my peers got to move forward in relationships and careers and finances, when there I hung from that bar. It's tough not to develop a victim mentality when you become fooled into believing you're stuck with an unbalanced life.

We all encounter troubles we can't avoid that leave us wondering if we have experienced our last drop of joy. Those times require that we work toward balance in whatever small ways we can and pray that God will steady us or the circumstances.

But for the majority of time when we're not weighed down by unusual demands, we need to take an assertive role and reassess how we're distributing our resources.

King Solomon had some incredible insights about a balanced life, learned the hard way after years of too much extreme living for his own good. We'll get to him again in the final chapter, but his life is worth a double study, so here's the first part.

He was a guy to envy. He had power, wealth, sex, and smarts. However, he let certain areas grow out of control, and those parts eventually choked his vitality.

He started out with a bang. As successor to the throne of Israel, he pleased God by asking for wisdom to do his job well. In return, God blessed him with a few other perks:

> God replied, "Because you have asked for wisdom in governing my people with justice and have not asked for a long life or wealth or the death of your enemies—I will give you what you asked for! I will give you a wise and understanding heart such as no one else has had or ever will have! And I will also give you what you did not ask for—riches and fame! No other king in all the world will be compared to you for the rest of your life! And if you follow me and obey my decrees and my commands as your father, David, did, I will give you a long life" (1 Kings 3:11-14).

Prosperity marked Solomon's reign. First Kings 4:20 says the people were happy and content. That chapter goes on to describe more details of his empire.

> The daily food requirements for Solomon's palace were 150 bushels of choice flour and 300 bushels of meal; also 10 oxen from the fattening pens, 20 pasture-fed cattle, 100 sheep or goats, as well as deer, gazelles, roe deer, and choice poultry. Solomon's dominion extended over all the kingdoms west of the Euphrates River, from Tiphsah to Gaza. And there was peace on all his borders (verses 22-24).

Sounds like the makings of an amazing life. Yet Solomon discovered that life overdone can topple hard.

We all have our unique weaknesses, areas we're prone to overdo. Solomon's were wealth and women. He had quite the harem, and he gathered them from pagan nations. That was a big no-no for God's people, who were to stick with God-followers as partners.

For all his abundance, he began to focus more on it than on the Giver of it. Too much was too much. Too much time spent on too many temporary attractions left Solomon with too little energy for God. As a result, he looked back and grieved the imbalance. All the material perks and worldly desires anyone could want still left him wanting. His lifestyle was out of sync with God.

There's nothing wrong with abundance. Abundance isn't even the point. God granted the blessings for Solomon to enjoy. However, excess of anything in human hands will lead to destruction when we don't offer our lives back to God, who coaches us on maintaining balance. Excess can include unhealthy habits, attitudes, relationship patterns, and on and on. It also includes obsessing about the things we think we lack.

The book of Ecclesiastes is pretty much 12 chapters of Solomon's regrets for how he had gotten off course. Note how jaded he had become:

> I said to myself, "Come on, let's try pleasure. Let's look for the 'good things' in life." But I found that this, too, was meaningless...After much thought, I decided to cheer myself with wine. And while still seeking wisdom, I clutched at foolishness...I also tried to find meaning by building huge homes for myself and by planting beautiful vineyards. I made gardens and parks, filling them with all kinds of fruit trees. I built reservoirs to collect the water to irrigate my many flourishing groves. I bought slaves, both men and women, and others were born into my house-hold...I collected great sums of silver and gold...I hired wonderful singers...and had many beautiful concubines. I had everything a man could desire! So I became greater than all who had lived in Jerusalem before me...Anything I wanted, I would take...I even found great pleasure in hard work, a reward for all my labors. But as I looked at everything I had worked so hard to accomplish, it was all so meaningless—like chasing the wind. There was nothing

really worthwhile anywhere...I came to hate all my hard
work here on earth, for I must leave to others everything
I have earned. How meaningless! So I gave up in despair
(Ecclesiastes 2:1-11, 18-20).

That from the guy to envy. He was viewed as great, but he felt
lousy. He realized the hard way that wealth and women and prestige
and power weren't enough. When his earthly status symbols tipped
the balance beam of life, his relationship with God teetered and fell
flat. Solomon didn't always apply the wisdom and understanding God
granted him. He found out in the end that striving apart from God
left him empty, with no medals to show for it.

So does that mean we're not supposed to give it all we've got? We're
not supposed to desire things or work hard to enjoy this life, even if
it is only a few decades long? What does a life look like that balances
the issues of our time on earth with seeking God for eternity? And
how do we figure it out before we get out of sync?

Well, Solomon eventually came to a conclusion about how to balance his priorities.

Ecclesiastes 11:9 (CEV) warns us to "Be cheerful and enjoy life while
you are young! Do what you want and find pleasure in what you see.
But don't forget that God will judge you for everything you do."

There you go. In a nutshell, God gives us freedom to make our
decisions, but balance weighs the outcomes against God's standards.
Here's a bit of what he wants from us:

He wants us to work hard...as we also make time for rest (Proverbs
12:11; Matthew 11:28-30).

He wants us to show mercy...as we stand up for truth (Matthew
5:7; Jude 1:3).

He wants us to focus on heaven...as we're making the most of our
days on earth (Matthew 6:19-21; Hebrews 12:1).

Solomon goes on to say, "Remember also your Creator in the days
of your youth" (Ecclesiastes 12:1 ESV). Can you hear his wise old
voice, intoning with slow thoughtfulness? His words ring true over the

changing times, for really, years may pass, but the story of life doesn't change much from generation to generation. We're all figuring out the same things about ourselves and God that Solomon and his peers dealt with in times past.

These transition years of early adulthood are filled with confusion because they're filled with so many changes and options and decisions. Sometimes it's enough to thwart the most valiant attempt to maintain stability and common sense. Some days you might feel as though your opportunities are limitless, other days as if you're spinning circles over the high bar.

It's about moderation. It's about not missing the best because of the so-so or even the good. When I was at my most burned out, I wasn't doing anything we usually think of as wrong. I was doing good things, working hard to earn a living, trying to seek God and be kind to those around me. But I was done. Emptied. I wonder now how I could have spared myself months of depression and despair if I would have let myself reach my limits sooner instead of trying to be a hero and handle it all. I didn't have to tackle the world all at once. There's simply no time for it.

Life is about seeking our Creator, who is able to lead us on a balanced course. He can steady us in any circumstance and let us know when we need to reshuffle our priorities. Even when our situation seems to get the best of us, he can calm us deep inside in ways we can't explain, except to say it's a God thing. With him as our coach and focal point, the world around us can spin and flip-flop all it wants to without making us sick with dizziness.

Seek your Creator today, and let him rescue you from the high bar of imbalanced living. Balance is not just for gymnasts. Recognize its worth, and watch your heart thrive with purpose and your days with meaning.

Put your hope in the LORD. Travel steadily
along his path. He will honor you.

PSALM 37:34

CONSIDER THIS...

1. Have you ever thought much about balance? In what ways do you see people living out of balance? How do their lives and families suffer because of it? Have you ever known someone who is book smart but lacking in wisdom, leaving a trail of bad decisions behind him or her? How do education and intelligence not necessarily ensure wise living?

2. What does balance look like in your life? Do you know certain telltale signs to recognize it in yourself? What areas might you need to improve?

3. Read Ecclesiastes 7:8 about the importance of finishing well. How might living a balanced life now extend the quality of your life into your later years? What current habits of yours fall into the category of starting well?

4. Check out these verses on steadiness: Job 4:4; Psalm 37:23; 40:2; James 1:5-8. Whose lives do you influence? How does your stability and balanced perspective affect those people? What are some characteristics of a person who keeps God as his or her ultimate stability?

5. Satisfaction in God leads to balanced living, because when we're fulfilled deep down in the soul, we'll remain steady through changing circumstances. Psalm 119:169,171,173-76 (MSG) are great verses to study and pray over for life.

> Let my cry come right into your presence, GOD; provide me with the insight that comes only from your Word...Let

praise cascade off my lips; after all, you've taught me the truth about life!...Put your hand out and steady me since I've chosen to live by your counsel...I love it when you show yourself! Invigorate my soul so I can praise you well, use your decrees to put iron in my soul. And should I wander off like a lost sheep—seek me! I'll recognize the sound of your voice.

So powerful! How can you apply these verses to your life?

20

WELCOME TO THE MOMENT;
IT'S DISAPPEARING FAST.

If we could jump ahead 50 or 60 years and see what our lives amount to, would it change how we spend our minutes today? I wonder how often I'd answer yes to that question.

While the future may appear as a never-ending road of possibilities while we're on the early side of life, time is limited and it passes swiftly. Right now will never happen again.

I thought about that recently as I looked through my parents' box of slides from when my brother, sisters, and I were kids, back in the Dark Ages before digital cameras. I brought the slides to Arkansas when I married and moved here with the intention of cataloguing them and making copies of my favorites. Several years later I finally got around to tackling the project.

For a week I spent evenings holding the small photos to the light. It was surreal looking at images that have been filed in my subconscious for decades. Family vacations, school events, ballet recitals, holidays, relatives, homes, neighbors…a dozen or so carousels holds a lot of memories. I couldn't shake the nostalgia that came over me knowing those moments caught on film were gone forever.

It also struck me how oblivious I was to the fleeting quality of each snapshot at the time it happened. Of course, I was a kid, and what child would think of that? However, my adult moments are passing just the same. Am I clued in yet to how preciously brief they all are? More important, how am I spending them?

Over the months of soul searching about these 20 insights I wish I'd known sooner, I've spent a boatload of mental energy replaying my life. It's been humbling.

We're granted only so much time on earth. It seems endless from a youthful perspective, but in my midthirties I'm already catching myself saying things like, I can't believe how quickly the year is flying. When did it get to be March? June? Another December?

And when did I become a thirtysomething?

I feel old. It has me scratching my head, wondering what happened to the last 15 years—and wondering if I made the most of that decade and a half.

We already delved into some of the reasons Solomon spent his later years bemoaning his younger years. Although he had many successes, he also had to live with regrets for ways he failed to apply the great wisdom God gave him. Only he and God knew how many opportunities he missed by not living up to his highest purpose. His heartache comes through loud and clear in his echoed words: "Meaningless! Meaningless!…Utterly meaningless! Everything is meaningless" (Ecclesiastes 1:2 NIV).

Asking for wisdom was great, but applying it consistently would have been better. He realized with 20/20 hindsight that nothing about this life lasts unless God is in the center of it.

> No matter how much we see, we are never satisfied. No matter how much we hear, we are not content…I devoted myself to search for understanding and to explore by wisdom everything being done under heaven…I observed everything going on under the sun, and really, it is all

meaningless—like chasing the wind. What is wrong cannot be made right. What is missing cannot be recovered. I said to myself, "Look, I am wiser than any of the kings who ruled in Jerusalem before me. I have greater wisdom and knowledge than any of them." So I set out to learn everything from wisdom to madness and folly. But I learned firsthand that pursuing all this is like chasing the wind (Ecclesiastes 1:8,13-17).

Notice he refers to everything done under heaven, going on under the sun. The things we do on earth that leave God and heaven out of the picture don't fulfill us long term. He goes on to say, "Who can eat or enjoy anything apart from [God]?" (Ecclesiastes 2:25).

In the end Solomon gained a deeper wisdom he lacked while young. He came to understand how each moment we live matters to God. Our priorities, our pastimes, our passions, our purpose. I wonder how he would have lived if he'd been able to recapture the moments that flew by while he wasn't making the most of them for God's purposes. His story makes me sad, but it also alerts me to how I spend my time here.

In contrast to Solomon and his regrets stands another biblical character whose story I'd like to emulate: Daniel, a man who made God his driving force and ultimate passion. Although Solomon was known for being the wisest in his time, Daniel stands out to me as someone who put wisdom into action.

In an age when putting God first meant taking your life in your hands, Daniel did not crumble. He invited God to live and breathe through his every word and action. Like Solomon, Daniel had a lot going for him. He was one of the Israelites taken captive to Babylon after King Nebuchadnezzar invaded Jerusalem. Although he was not in a position of power when we meet him in the book of Daniel, his character earned him the respect of kings. He grew up in an important family, and because of his background, his looks, and his education, he was chosen to serve in the palace and learn the Babylonian language and writings.

He and the other young men with him were offered rations of fine food, same as the king ate. However, unlike Solomon, Daniel set himself apart for God by refraining from the pagan lifestyle. God took that act of loyalty and made Daniel thrive.

> God gave [Daniel] an unusual aptitude for understanding every aspect of literature and wisdom. And God gave Daniel the special ability to interpret the meanings of visions and dreams...Whenever the king consulted [him] in any matter requiring wisdom and balanced judgment, he found [him] ten times more capable than any of the magicians and enchanters in his entire kingdom (Daniel 1:17,20).

When Nebuchadnezzar threatened to kill his advisors if they couldn't interpret a dream, Daniel prayed for God's intervention and experienced supernatural insight no human could conjure. As God worked miraculously through Daniel, Daniel pointed each success back to God, giving praise where it was due:

> During the night God explained the secret to Daniel in a vision. Then Daniel praised the God of heaven. Daniel said: "Praise God forever and ever, because he has wisdom and power...He gives wisdom to those who are wise and knowledge to those who understand. He makes known secrets that are deep and hidden; he knows what is hidden in darkness, and light is all around him. I thank you and praise you, God of my ancestors, because you have given me wisdom and power" (Daniel 2:19-23 NCV).

Daniel served four kings in his lifetime and went on to star in the famous story of the lions' den (chapter 6). From all accounts we see him filling each moment with meaning and leaving powerful people mesmerized by the God he lived for. He didn't wait for stupendous circumstances. He was a captive with no choice but to serve. But he didn't let a rough road deny him from living out his God-given purpose; he served God, and he did it with the integrity of a spiritual prince.

Although he was born and died long before this verse was written, he exemplified its message: "Whatever you do, work heartily, as for the Lord" (Colossians 3:23 ESV). I think it's safe to say that if Daniel ever saw a box of slides from his life, regret wouldn't eat at him the way it did Solomon. From what we know of him, I can't see Daniel grieving missed opportunities, because he seemed to make the most of all of them.

Unlike Solomon and his view that life is meaningless, Daniel packed eternal meaning into his days on earth. This life does mean something for eternity, whether we live like it or not. We will miss the deeper meaning if we're wrapped up in our own thing.

What about you? What will this moment lived in your twenties mean for your eternity?

As you take each next step on your journey mapped out by the God who loves you, know that you are not alone in the challenges. Life is hard, but it is good. Don't settle for the meaningless path that lives only for this passing earth.

I've wondered who you are, who out there might pick up this book someday. Whatever your name, whatever your situation, feel prayed over because you have been. May it cause your heart to smile knowing that a stranger in Arkansas has been holding your heart toward heaven, asking that our great God would make himself obvious to you.

I feel giddy imagining how he uses each prayer we utter, awestruck by the connection we have with each other who know Jesus as Savior. Thank you for taking time to read a few hindsights I wish I'd known. If even one line sparked your curiosity for God and his Word, then I will consider this a Daniel project, every word typed with a purpose that extends beyond my life.

Years from now, when I think back to the hours spent lingering over the keyboard, willing *something* to show up on the screen, I will pray again for you, because...

> I couldn't stop thanking God for you—every time I prayed,
> I'd think of you and give thanks. But I do more than

thank. I ask—ask the God of our Master, Jesus Christ, the God of glory—to make you intelligent and discerning in knowing him personally, your eyes focused and clear, so that you can see exactly what it is he is calling you to do, grasp the immensity of this glorious way of life he has for his followers, oh, the utter extravagance of his work in us who trust him—endless energy, boundless strength! (Ephesians 1:16-19 MSG).

There's an opportunity coming your way soon. Every second holds great potential for growth and for making a difference. Someday you will see a slide show of your life. Will you be filled with nostalgia over memories spent with your Savior, or will you grieve what can never be redone? When you commit to God's purposes, you won't miss the adventure that goes beyond your hopes and dreams.

No regret.

No wasted time.

No holding back.

With all this going for us, my dear, dear friends, stand your ground. And don't hold back. Throw yourself into the work of the Master, confident that nothing you do for him is a waste of time or effort.

1 Corinthians 15:58 MSG

CONSIDER THIS...

1. Gut check: If you were to see a slide show in heaven of the past month of your life, would you feel nostalgic or regretful? How about the past week? Today? The past hour?

2. What do you think of Solomon's view that life is meaningless?

What gives meaning to your life? Consider what your life means to God. Is your view in line with his?

3. I love these verses!

> Teach us how short our lives really are so that we may be wise...Fill us with your love every morning. Then we will sing and rejoice all our lives...Show your servants the wonderful things you do; show your greatness to their children. Lord our God, treat us well. Give us success in what we do; yes, give us success in what we do (Psalm 90:12-17 NCV).

What does success look like to you? How does your definition steer your purpose?

4. We all have days when our best efforts seem futile for anything worthwhile. How does 1 Corinthians 15:58 give you hope that, whether or not you see success today, God will make your work for him count? In Acts 20:24, Paul minces no words about his single-minded devotion to Christ. Does this verse cause you to cringe or cheer? Why?

5. Proverbs is another book that King Solomon wrote. Read Proverbs 3:5-26. What are some benefits of gaining wisdom? We all get off track spiritually from time to time when our humanness hollers for too much attention. What attitude should we have toward God's discipline for getting us back on track with his purposes?

And Then Some

GET INSPIRED:
QUICK-REFERENCE SCRIPTURES

Anxiety/Worry
Matthew 6:33-34
Luke 12:22-26
Philippians 4:6-7

Attitude
Proverbs 14:30
Ephesians 4:22-24
Philippians 2:5-8

Emotions
Proverbs 4:23

Faith
Psalm 46:10
Jeremiah 17:7
Matthew 14:28-31
Mark 9:23
Luke 12:27-28
Hebrews 11:1,6

Fear
Deuteronomy 31:6,8
Isaiah 43:1-5
Hebrews 13:5-6

Forgiveness
Psalm 103:3
Isaiah 1:18
Colossians 1:13-14
Colossians 3:12-13

Future
Isaiah 46:4
Jeremiah 29:11-13

God's Presence
Psalm 142:3
Psalm 145:17-19
John 14:18

God's Provision
Psalm 23
Psalm 84:11
Psalm 85:12
Psalm 145:19
John 10:10

God's Love
Psalm 136
Psalm 145:8-9
Jeremiah 31:3-4
John 3:16
Ephesians 3:16-21
1 John 3:16
1 John 4:19

God's Voice
1 Kings 19:11-12
Job 37:5
Psalm 95:6-7

God's Will
Mark 3:33-35
Romans 8:27-28
Romans 12:1-2

Gratitude
Psalm 136
1 Thessalonians 5:18

Healing
Exodus 15:26
Psalm 103:3
Malachi 4:2

Holy Spirit
John 14:16-17,26
John 15:26
Romans 8:5-9
Romans 8:26-27
1 Thessalonians 5:19

Hope
Psalm 25:4-5
Psalm 42:5
Proverbs 10:28
Proverbs 13:12

Humility
2 Samuel 22:28
Luke 18:14
Ephesians 4:2

Joy
Joel 2:21
Philippians 4:4
1 Thessalonians 5:16
1 Peter 1:6

Judgmental Spirit
Matthew 7:1-5

Knowing God
Hosea 6:3
Ephesians 3:16-21

Living for God
Psalm 139:23-24
Psalm 141:4
Proverbs 3:1-6
Galatians 6:9
Ephesians 4:1
Colossians 3:23-24
Hebrews 10:35-39

Hebrews 12:1-3

Past
Isaiah 43:18-19
Ephesians 4:22-24

Peace
John 14:27
Philippians 4:6-7,9
Colossians 3:15

Praise/Worship
Psalm 8
Psalm 13:5-6
Psalm 107:8-9
Psalms 147–150

Prayer
Psalm 5:1-3
Daniel 9:17-18
Matthew 7:7-11
Luke 11:5-13
1 Thessalonians 5:17
James 5:16

Purity
Proverbs 4:24-27
Ezekiel 36:26
Matthew 5:8
Philippians 4:8
2 Timothy 2:20-22

Relationships
Matthew 7:12
Luke 10:27
1 Thessalonians 5:12-13
1 John 3:16

Salvation
Jonah 2:9
John 3:16
Ephesians 2:8-9
Revelation 7:10

Sin
Isaiah 1:18
Romans 3:23
Romans 5:8
Romans 6:23
1 John 1:8

Speech
Exodus 4:12
Proverbs 18:21
Proverbs 29:20
Ephesians 4:29
Colossians 4:6
James 3:2

Strength
Joshua 1:9
Isaiah 30:15

Waiting
Psalm 27:14
Psalm 40:1
Isaiah 40:31 (NASB)

Wisdom
Job 28:28
Proverbs 2:1-5
Micah 6:9

MAKE IT MATTER

Random Suggestions for Living Abundantly

1. Send a thank-you note to someone just for being in your life.

2. Drop off magazines at nursing homes (the more recent the better).

3. Clean your parents' windows.

4. Smile at the cashier.

5. Learn about missions work at church.

6. Send a note of appreciation to your pastor.

7. Take a blooming plant to a lonely neighbor.

8. Smile in the middle of a bad mood.

9. Eat something healthy.

10. Take a walk.

11. Research a vacation spot.

12. Thank God for your friends.

13. Memorize a Bible verse.

14. Read something educational.

15. Pay the toll for the person behind you.

16. Mow someone else's yard.

17. Shovel someone else's driveway.

18. Sing in your vehicle.

19. Put a favorite quote on your windowsill.

20. Hug someone (make sure you know them!).

21. Read a chapter in the Old Testament and one in the New Testament.

22. Smile up toward Jesus.

23. Watch the breeze flutter the leaves.

24. Take your shoes off and wiggle your toes.

25. Stretch.

26. Nurture a houseplant.

27. Buy something on clearance.

28. Put money, even $1, into savings.

29. Dream about your life ten years from now.

30. Imagine yourself without television.

31. Go a night without television.

32. Pick a life's Bible verse.

33. Thank God for music.

34. Ask God to reveal who you influence.

35. Rearrange your furniture.

36. Say people's names when you greet them.

37. Buy fresh flowers for your home or office.

38. Be amazed by the familiarity of your hands and feet; thank God they're yours.

39. Sing "Jesus Loves Me."

40. Spend an hour at the library.

41. Discover a favorite healthy snack.

42. Clean something.

43. Journal.

44. Donate.

45. Volunteer.

46. Talk to God about your day.

47. Consider pursuing the career of your heart.

48. Tell your family members you love them.

49. Decorate for the next holiday.

50. Learn the meaning of Advent.

51. Research your town's history.

52. Count the varieties of animals you see in one day.

53. Count the number of children you see in one day.

54. Refuse to complain for one day.

55. Contact someone you haven't seen for a while.

56. Sit in a warm bath.

57. Try a new form of exercise.

58. Take a nap.

59. Look at the stars.

60. Go to bed early.

61. Discover the perks of early morning.

62. Give someone the benefit of the doubt.

63. Ignore a current worry for one whole day.

64. Thank God for your teachers.

65. Make a list of your favorite things.

66. Thank God for computer gurus.

67. Spend two hours near any body of water.

68. Read three psalms.

69. Get a flu shot.

70. Buy a new accessory.

71. Turn off your cell phone.

72. Forgive someone's mistake, including yours.

73. Call your parents.

74. Notice the sunset.

75. Leave work early.

76. Sleep in.

77. Wash your sheets and shower before bed.

78. Enjoy a comfort food.

79. Pray for five people other than yourself.

80. Listen for the birds.

81. Volunteer again.

82. Pray for the patient in the next ambulance you see.

83. Pray for the next driver who makes you mad.

84. Try a different church service.

85. Ask about current needs at church.

86. Think carefully about the hymn and chorus lyrics at church.

87. Pray about a newspaper headline.

88. Pray for the country's leaders.

89. Thank God for eternity.

90. Dream about heaven.

91. Commit to daily multivitamins.

92. Drink herbal tea instead.

93. Get a yearly doctor's exam.

94. Stop now for a drink of water.

95. Watch the clouds.

96. Stand in the rain.

97. Try a different soap or toothpaste.

98. Help a coworker.

99. Smile at your boss.

100. Ask God to make himself obvious to you today.

Things I Wish I'd Done More of Sooner

1. Traveled

2. Saved money

3. Bought furniture

4. Spent more time with grandparents

5. Volunteered

6. Established a workout habit

7. Used sunscreen

8. Ate healthy

9. Took more risks

10. Lived proactively

11. Committed everything to prayer

12. Invested

13. Let God have all of me

14. Splurged

15. Been more comfortable with myself

Things I Wish I'd Figured Out Sooner

1. Take career glitches in stride.

2. Early morning is amazing.

3. "Thinking too much" is overrated.

4. I am not a victim of my emotions.

5. Life will always be messier than I'd like.

6. Go to God first.

7. Not everyone thinks like I do.

8. Variety is the spice of life.

9. True love is not scientific.

10. Positive attitudes don't just happen.

11. Positive attitudes solve many problems.

12. Not everyone will like me.

13. Even fewer will love me.

14. God designed me for victory.

15. Life really is all about God and others.

Things I Wish I'd Seen as Handicaps Sooner

1. Worrying about a husband

2. Being insecure

3. Eating too much junk food

4. Being too hard on myself

5. Holding grudges

6. Waiting for someone to fix things

7. Complaining

8. Making snap judgments

9. Thinking negatively

10. Waiting for the perfect opportunity

11. Putting off until tomorrow

12. Thinking others have it better

13. Regretting the past

14. Wasting the present

15. Wishing on the future

Chapter 5—Dreams worth chasing are worth a long-distance run.

1. Max Lucado, *He Still Moves Stones* (Dallas, Texas: W Publishing Group, 1993), 76.

Chapter 13—Everyone has issues; own yours.

1. Oswald Chambers, *My Utmost for His Highest,* Christian Library ed. (Uhrichsville, Ohio: Barbour and Company, 1987), 33-34.

Chapter 15—Move beyond the pit of regret.

1. *Merriam-Webster's Collegiate Dictionary,* 11th ed. (Springfield, Massachusetts: Merriam-Webster, Inc., 2003), 1042.

About the Author

Erin Keeley Marshall was raised in Chicago's western suburbs and graduated cum laude from Taylor University in 1994 with a bachelor's in English writing and a mass communications minor.

She has more than a decade of editorial and writing experience, cutting her teeth as a freelance copy editor and proofreader before joining Tyndale House Publishers in 1998, where she worked for several years.

Marriage in 2003 brought her to northwest Arkansas, where she writes and edits while gazing out the window at cliffs and water and trees and mama deer with their spotted fawns—a dream environment for the creative juices. Her first novel, *The Bluff Dweller,* earned third place in the Women's Fiction category for the American Christian Fiction Writers' Genesis 2006 contest.

She is an active member of a nondenominational, Bible-based congregation of several thousand in one of the fastest-growing regions of the country. She has written for a number of church publications and has been part of the women's ministries leadership team.

Visit Erin's website at www.erinkeeleymarshall.net.

Other Good
Harvest House Reading

THE WOMAN I AM BECOMING
T. Suzanne Eller

This honest, faith-filled look at the journey to maturity helps 18- to 29-year-old women explore key questions: What is a *real* woman? What should I look like? Who should I be with? What about *my* faith? Each short chapter offers personal application, real-life advice, and questions.

DATING WITH PURE PASSION
Rob Eagar

With his compelling personal testimony and thoroughly scriptural teaching, Rob Eagar encourages readers to stop chasing romance and sex and to pursue their heart's deepest desire—the truly passionate love of Jesus Christ.

JUST MARRIED
Margaret Feinberg

Just Married engagingly walks twentysomethings through their first years of marriage and tackles one of the biggest challenges for newlyweds—establishing their relationships with God both as individuals and as a married couple.

WHY GUYS NEED GOD
Michael Erre

Is the Christian community doing a good job of presenting the message of Jesus in a compelling way to men? Pastor Mike Erre rejects cultural definitions of masculinity and offers a thoroughly biblical and engaging theology of manhood that is missing in many churches today.

WINDOWS INTO THE HEART OF GOD
Preston Parrish

When we draw near to Jesus, amazing things happen. In *Windows into the Heart of God*, you will take a 31-day journey that encourages, builds up, and challenges you to flourish in their personal relationship with the Lord Jesus Christ—a journey that will leave you forever changed!

HARVEST HOUSE
PUBLISHERS